"Because we cannot all enroll in Linn Marie Tonstad's Queer Theology seminar, we owe it to ourselves, and to the vitality of queer theology itself, to read—and re-read—this book so we can learn from the one of its best practitioners the radical art of queer theological truth-telling."

**—Kent Brintnall**
Associate Professor, University of North Carolina at Charlotte

"Linn Tonstad is the best queer theologian of her generation, and she has written a superb introduction to the field. Tonstad lucidly explicates, and she judges, pointing to the limitations of queer theological projects that are insufficiently intersectional in their analysis as well as the possibilities being unleashed by a younger generation of queer theologians who adamantly refuse heteropatriarchy, racism, colonialism, and capitalism—all the while taking Christian traditions seriously."

**—Vincent Lloyd**
Associate Professor, Villanova University

"In this brilliant burst of theological becoming, Linn Tonstad leads us beyond liberal apologetics for sexual difference. Queer Theology reveals something indispensable and yet irreducible to theology itself: arching between desire and death, theology here faces its deformations and unleashes its transformations. Vibrantly engaging her students as well as her theorists, the text queers the deep questions of Christianity."

**—Catherine Keller**
Professor, Drew University, The Theological School

"At last, a truly helpful introduction to a hotly contested notion: 'queer theology.' Tonstad clarifies in graceful prose the limitations, stakes, and pleasures of what could be queer in Christian theology. Timely and long overdue, this book will help students, queer theologians, and other theological adventurers recognize the far deeper challenges and possibilities that queer theologies beyond apology may offer to Christian understanding and justice-making efforts."

**—Laurel C. Schneider**
Professor, Vanderbilt University

"This pacey, accessible introduction steers a course adroitly through queer theology's choppy waters without flattening out its complexities. Tonstad orients readers to theological and cultural markers they will recognize, and lucidly outlines some emerging developments in the field."

**—Susannah Cornwall**
Lecturer, University of Exeter, United Kingdom

# QUEER
# THEOLOGY

# CASCADE COMPANIONS

The Christian theological tradition provides an embarrassment of riches: from Scripture to modern scholarship, we are blessed with a vast and complex theological inheritance. And yet this feast of traditional riches is too frequently inaccessible to the general reader.

The Cascade Companions series addresses the challenge by publishing books that combine academic rigor with broad appeal and readability. They aim to introduce nonspecialist readers to that vital storehouse of authors, documents, themes, histories, arguments, and movements that comprise this heritage with brief yet compelling volumes.

TITLES IN THIS SERIES:

# QUEER
# THEOLOGY

*Beyond Apologetics*

## LINN MARIE TONSTAD

 CASCADE *Books* · Eugene, Oregon

QUEER THEOLOGY
Beyond Apologetics

Cascade Companions 40

Cascade Books
An Imprint of Wipf and Stock Publishers
199 W. 8th Ave., Suite 3
Eugene, OR 97401

www.wipfandstock.com

PAPERBACK ISBN: 978-1-4982-1879-5
HARDCOVER ISBN: 978-1-4982-1881-8
EBOOK ISBN: 978-1-4982-1880-1

### *Cataloguing-in-Publication data:*

Names: Tonstad, Linn Marie, author.

Title: Queer theology : beyond apologetics / by Linn Marie Tonstad.

Description: Eugene, OR : Cascade Books, 2018. | Cascade Companions 40 | Includes bibliographical references.

Identifiers: ISBN 978-1-4982-1879-5 (paperback). | ISBN 978-1-4982-1881-8 (hardcover). | ISBN 978-1-4982-1880-1 (ebook).

Subjects: LCSH: Homosexuality—Religious aspects—Christianity. | Liberation theology. | Theology.

Classification: BR115 H6 T65 2018 (paperback) | BR115 (epub).

Manufactured in the U.S.A.                    02/22/19

# CONTENTS

1

# WHAT IS QUEER THEOLOGY?

WHAT IS QUEER THEOLOGY? And what does queer have
to do with Christianity?[1] Different answers to these questions often reflect disagreement about what queer means,
and so about what queering Christianity would require.
Much of what gets called queer theology in Christianity
is theology that in some way is *about* queer people—that
is, people who identify and understand themselves either
as persons whose sexuality is not wholly heterosexual, or

1. These questions are the focus of this book. The lines between
theology, theory, Christianity, not Christianity, religion, not religion,
queer, not queer, are always contested. Many forms of queer theology and queer religion aren't Christian and don't want to be. Some
emerge from different religions, while others are concerned with
spirituality more generally or want to move away from identification
with any particular tradition. Using Christianity in the singular, as I
do here, is also misleading. There are always only Christianities.

whose gender is not the one assigned by medical authorities at birth, or of course both.

*Terminological note: In this book, trans\* is shorthand for various forms of trans identification and experience. Trans\* can indicate someone who was assigned male at birth, but who is female or vice versa, or someone who identifies specifically as trans (without transitioning to a particular gender), or as gender-nonconforming. Trans\* identification is possible regardless of whether or not one transitions socially or medically.*

*In ancient Rome, there was a geographic distinction between trans-alpine Gaul and cis-alpine Gaul. Trans-alpine Gaul was on the other side of the Alps, while cis-alpine Gaul was on the same side as Rome. In analogy to this distinction, saying that someone is cis means that they identify with the gender assigned to them at birth. Many gender-nonconforming people identify as trans\*, but some do not.*

*Other terms that indicate nonnormative gender identification or performance include nonbinary (neither male nor female in a binary way; maybe more female on one day and more male on another, or neither all the time), agender (having no gender), and genderqueer (not captured by stable gender categories). Intersex people, whose genital morphology and/or chromosomes trouble binary gender identification, have different and often ambivalent relationships to gender nonnormativity. These categories shift as people take up and discard language as it works or ceases to work for them. Sexual and gender minorities have long histories of inventing language according to need, and leaving it behind when it becomes less useful. This book tries to avoid excessively fixing language, as if getting language right were equivalent to doing justice. The book takes for granted that people should be referred to in whatever way they prefer, using whatever terms make sense for them.*

*The book's most controversial terminology is that of "queer," a term many sexual and gender minorities do not use. In my queer theology classes, I have students who identify only as lesbian, straight, homosexual, asexual, or trans\*, as well as students who find that "queer" is a word that works for them. Because this book makes the argument that queer theology is not about apologetics for the inclusion of sexual and gender minorities in Christianity, but about visions of sociopolitical transformation that alter practices of distinction harming gender and sexual minorities as well as many other minoritized populations, queer is a reasonably (in)adequate term to use.*

For many, queer theology indicates theologies in which 1) sexuality and gender are discussed 2) in ways that affirm, represent, or apologize for queer persons. I teach a seminar called Queer Theology, and most of my students show up on the first day assuming that the semester will be spent reading texts that explain why and how Christianity and queerness become compatible—how persons who are gay, lesbian, bisexual, or trans\* may be included into Christianity. They assume that there *are* ways to include LGBT persons into Christianity by affirming relationships between persons of the same gender and allowing trans\* people to participate fully in the life of the church, but that arguments and examples are needed to justify those practices of inclusion. Those arguments are needed because so many Christians are hostile to LGBTQIA persons,[2] but

2. There are a variety of acronyms in use to avoid the cumbersome nature of specifying everything one means in contexts where preferred terminology is often shifting. LGBTQIA stands for lesbian, gay, bisexual, trans, queer, intersex, and asexual. Some add a P for pansexual or an O for omnisexual. Others like QUILTBAG (queer/questioning, uncertain, intersex, lesbian, trans\*, bisexual, asexual, gay/genderqueer). While homosexual is often used in hostile ways by church authorities, some gay people reclaim it as a

also because my students tend to share the sense many Christians have: that sexual ethics are fundamental to Christianity, and that figuring out what sexual acts are permitted (licit) is an important, indeed central task of living a Christian life. If we imagine sexual ethics as a search for the permitted and the forbidden, queer theology would then be about finding ways to move (mostly monogamous, married) same-sex relationships from the column of sexual acts marked "illicit" (forbidden) to the column marked "licit" (permitted).

Students often come to my class having already encountered some of the most popular apologetic strategies in queer theology, strategies that we examine in the next chapter. Apologetics is one of the oldest forms of Christian speech, developed in early Christianity in a context in which many intellectuals in the surrounding culture thought Christian claims about God's presence in Jesus Christ (incarnation) and Christ's resurrection from the dead were silly and unlikely claims. Many philosophers and theologians believed that the aim of existence should be to be freed from the body and its limitations, because the body subjects us to change and death. What's more, God is not matter but spirit; indeed, God is as different from matter as can be imagined, because matter has a beginning and an end, and matter always changes, while God neither has a beginning nor an end, nor does God change. So how could God be "incarnated" in a human being, who is born

---

political designation. Until the early 1970s, many US-American lesbians would have called themselves gay women, or simply said that they were "in the life." Some lesbians prefer to identify as dykes. Within queer culture, there are various ways to indicate the complexities of gender and sexuality, including terms like butch, femme, masc, MOC (masculine of center), boi, Aggressive, Two-Spirit, butch queen, femme queen, stud, and (many, many) more.

*of a woman*, dies, and changes throughout life? How silly it would be even to suggest such a thing!

Christians developed apologetic strategies in response to such skepticism: arguments for the plausibility of Christian claims and ways of interpreting the world. Such arguments usually had to rely on at least some assumptions that were shared between Christians and their critics; otherwise, what would convince the critic that Christian claims were likely ways of understanding God's relationship to the world? Christian apologists would identify assumptions that Christians and their critics shared (that God is spirit, not matter; God does not change; God is eternal) and then argue that such ways of understanding God were not contradicted by Christian claims regarding incarnation and God's presence in the person and body of Jesus Christ.

In similar ways, apologetic strategies in queer theology start from disagreement about whether Christianity can accept the full participation of persons in same-sex relationships and persons whose gender identity does not match the one assigned at birth by medical authorities. Many Christians believe that Christianity condemns any sexual relationships that take place outside of lifelong, legally recognized, monogamous, heterosexual marriages. Queer theologians and biblical scholars engaged in apologetics look for ways to counter such claims so that, at a minimum, Christian churches will be willing to accept marriage between persons of the same sex and affirm the gender identity of all persons. At least for the purposes of argument, queer apologists share many of the assumptions held by those who believe that Christianity has no room for sexual relationships between persons of the same sex, or for persons whose gender identity was wrongly assigned at birth. The most obvious shared assumption is that gender and sexuality *matter* theologically, *matter* Christianly, so to speak.

Why would one think that gender and sexuality matter Christianly? Many early Christian theologians believed that gender and sexuality were at best temporary accommodations for the purpose of producing enough people to fill up heaven with the appropriate number of inhabitants, rather than intrinsic, important, permanent parts of what it means to be human, as most people now believe. Some speculated that all the saved would become male in the life to come; others thought that gender would disappear completely. In the life to come, all would be perfect, Christians thought. Since women were sometimes taken to be defective men (lacking in enough heat and activity in the body), this would require them to become men. Or, since all would be perfect, they would be freed of the differences in bodily constitution that characterize humans in this life. Probably, Origen speculated, this would mean that all would become spherical, since clearly a sphere is the most perfect shape.

Because of the resurrection of Jesus, Christians had to (in strong disagreement with many of the surrounding intellectual cultures) affirm the resurrection of the body. The goal of perfected human existence was not to *escape* from the body, but to be resurrected with a *transformed* body: a body no longer subject to sin, death, and decay. We are often told that Christianity is hostile to the body, seeing it as something that has to be subdued and overcome rather than affirmed and enjoyed. But that is at best an oversimplification. Gregory of Nyssa's famous *On Virginity* points out that the best possible outcome of a long, happy marriage is that someone gets to watch their beloved die. This outcome is an inescapable part of life and, again, that's the *happiest* of endings. Placing all one's hopes for happiness in marriage thus leads, sooner or later but inevitably, to sadness, loss, and mourning. Instead, Gregory argues, Christians should seek their primary happiness in the only end that neither changes nor can be lost: God.

For many of us, there's something off here: isn't change an inevitable part of human existence? Isn't change *good*? In the thought-worlds within which Christianity arose, change was not necessarily, as many now assume, a neutral category: something just *changes*. In that context, most thinkers assumed that change was, inevitably, either for the better or the worse. If it was for the better, then what changed was clearly not as good as it could have been, since it was able to change for the better. If for the worse, then what changed was not as good as it should have been, since it was able to change for the worse. Obviously (to them), if something is good, it is better for it to last, rather than to disappear and be lost. But because of death, all human projects, desires, and hopes are ultimately futile, ending in loss. The only orientation of human existence that is not threatened by death is the orientation to that which is good in itself, life in itself, and everlasting, the same from age to age: God. Thus, all other goods have to be seen in their relative unimportance compared to God. That doesn't mean other goods are not important at all, but they are not important in comparison to God, since God is the only good that lasts forever and never disappoints or disappears.

In early Christianity, one way of living out that orientation in daily life was virginity, a symbolic way to embody an unchanging orientation to God that avoided the participation in the cycle of birth (and so death and loss) that marriage and (especially) children entail. Marriage was often taken to be at best an accommodation to the intensity of sexual desire many experience; the more perfect state would be the unchanging orientation of virginity. The combined consequence of all this, in very general terms, was that at best, lifelong, "heterosexual," monogamous marriage was an accommodation to human weakness, not the ideal Christian state. Apologetic strategies in early Christianity were, thus, primarily concerned to justify just how highly Christianity *valued* the body, rather than appropriately subduing and despising it, as many of the dominant philosophies argued one ought. Christians shared with the surrounding intellectual cultures the general sense that God's incarnation (in *caro*, in flesh—the origin of our word carnivorous) in the body was, considered abstractly, an implausible event. Rather than a degradation of God, Christians argued, the incarnation was the sanctification of the flesh, of the body, through an unfathomable act of divine mercy and generosity. God *irreversibly* joins Godself to that which is very unlike God: material creation—specifically, a human body. In that joining, material creation is transformed, but not escaped or left behind.

Contemporary queer apologists find much in these Christian histories to criticize, and much to affirm. The transformations in cultural and Christian sensibilities (to the extent that those can be distinguished) regarding the body, gender, and sexuality in the intervening centuries are significant. We should note just how far from contemporary Christian worries about sexuality many of these concerns are. The idea that God's plan for humanity is a lifelong union between a man and a woman means little in the kind of context we have just described. More faithfully to their concerns, we might say something like the following: God's plan for humanity is their salvation and sanctification from subjection to death and corruption. Take, for example, the apostle Paul, who is held responsible for some of the attitudes toward sex that many contemporary Christians disagree with. While he makes occasional comments about marriage and properly gendered behavior, such issues are not even remotely close to what he sees as the heart of the gospel. In 1 Cor 15:3–7, he reminds the Corinthians of what he taught them—which was what he in turn had been taught: that Christ died for sin like scripture said, that he was buried and raised on the third day, and that he appeared to various disciples (and finally to Paul). He then turns to what he sees as a, or maybe *the*, crucial issue: "the last enemy to be destroyed is death" (1 Cor 15:26).

The idea that death—*death* as such, not just untimely deaths caused by injustice, cancer, police violence, war, or accidents—is a problem is not one that enjoys a great deal of cultural currency in the West today, except perhaps in the circles that imagine technological life-enhancement to include the singularity, or the capacity to download one's consciousness onto a computer and thus continue to live forever or for a very long time in a different form of embodiment. Philosophers and cultural interpreters have argued that the fear of death is at the heart of many of the ways in which human beings find themselves unable to live at peace with each other and with the world. Some philosophers and theologians argue that death is the horizon that gives meaning to life. Death gives life completion; from the perspective of death, life's futility and possible meaningfulness are both made evident. It is death that lends finality and weight to everything we do. The Catholic theologian Karl Rahner thought that giving oneself trustfully over to death is a way of giving oneself over trustfully to the dazzling mystery that is God, rather than clinging fearfully to the things of this life that inevitably disappoint. Feminists worry that fear of death leads to denial of death. Death follows birth, and most people who give birth are women. Women thus become more closely associated with finitude (limitation) and the body, and so associated with the devalued aspects of human existence: nature, the body, and our relative powerlessness and helplessness. The concerns that lead many early Christians to be suspicious of understanding oneself primarily as a sexual being no longer worry many Christians today in quite the same way. Instead, Christianity has a reputation for hating the body, valuing the soul over the body, and seeking to control the body by way of the soul.

There are two often-mentioned villains in this regard: Augustine and Descartes. Augustine thought that the disharmony between himself and his body was an expression of fallen human sinfulness. The body's desires are all over the place. "My" body does not conform to "my" desires. For instance, let's say that I want to become a better athlete. "I" decide to get up early tomorrow to train, but when my alarm rings, my body doesn't want to get up and go to the track. "I" have to subdue my body in order to achieve the end I want: to become a faster runner. Or, to choose a much more familiar Augustinian example: many of us may experience sexual desire for a variety of (often inappropriate) people at various (often inconvenient) times. For Augustine, this unruliness of the body (as he understood it) had a particular physiological expression: the fact that cis-male erections are not subject to the will. Erections arrive (or don't) whenever they want. The body thus makes apparent that "I" experience desires that "I" do not control. Paul's discussion in Romans 7 of not doing what he wants and doing what he does not want became a classic scriptural source describing this experience—an experience that is, in some ways, familiar to many of us, even if the psychology and concerns that explain that experience are different between our context, Paul's,[3] and Augustine's. "I" may want to be more disciplined about my training, but when it comes time to go to the gym, "I" decide to watch Netflix instead.

3. Many scholars today do not think that Paul is speaking in his own voice in this passage.

(Who is this "I," and which "I" am I?) We are, Augustine thought, divided against ourselves, and we need to remold ourselves to become unified, oriented toward the only good that never disappoints: God. As Augustine sighed to God, "My heart is restless until it rests in thee." Before the fall, Augustine thought, we would not have been so divided. We would have been united with ourselves in body, mind, and spirit. Our bodies would have conformed perfectly to our wills, which would have been determined by reason. Augustine imagined that the rational will would have oriented human desire and action. In other words, cis-men would have had full control of their erections.

Centuries later, René Descartes sat by a fire during a devastating European war, shivering and thinking. The world was collapsing around him. Was there anything about which he could be certain? How could he know that his experience of the world was real and true? Maybe he was sleeping, only dreaming that he was sitting by the fire. Or maybe he was being deceived by an evil demon who was giving him the impression that he was sitting by the fire thinking. But aha! as the story goes: He could be certain of one thing, and one thing only: *cogito, ergo sum*. I think, therefore I am. The "I" that doubts whether anything else it experiences is real, *must* therefore be real, even if nothing else is.[4] In the general outline of Western intellectual history, Descartes comes to stand in for two problems that characterize European colonialism and Christianity in modernity. One, an approach to the world in which the self stands at the center, and is certain, while everything else is

---

4. Often left out of the standard story is the very *next* thought that Descartes had: that he has the idea of a perfect being, God, and that he could never have come up with such an idea on his own. Therefore, it must have been placed in him by the perfect being, who therefore must exist.

not. And two, an approach to the self that fundamentally divides it between soul and body, where the self lives in the soul, which inhabits a body—but isn't, really, a body.[5] This "Cartesian" anthropology (a way of understanding the human being) becomes shorthand for referring to the ways in which modern, Western, white anthropology has gone awry.

Instead of recognizing the identity of the self with the body, and the mind with the brain, philosophers and theologians have imagined that there's something else that carries the identity of the human being: a rational mind irreducible to the brain, or a soul. The human person is imagined as divided between two different principles, with one of them (the soul) of more value and lastingness than the other (the body). The two are often thought to be in conflict: the body's unruly desires need to be subdued by the rational mind. To live in harmony with oneself is to live in such a way that the soul directs and rules the body. This dualistic anthropology leads to ranking people according to the extent to which they succeed in disciplining and distancing themselves from the body. The more rational are distinguished from the less rational, the more human from the less human. The more human, or fully human? The white, propertied, European, Christian (or, later, Enlightened) man, who subdued himself and his household (women, children, and servants) by way of his superior reason. The less human? Those who didn't own property, who weren't white, who weren't male, who weren't Christian or Enlightened.

This dualistic anthropology depended on two basic assumptions: one, human reason is formed in order to allow human beings to know themselves and the world in

5. Descartes famously speculated that soul and body were probably connected only by the pineal gland.

rational, objectively justifiable ways, and two, that rational mind is where human identity really lies. Rightly ordered reason can direct human desire; humans can know ourselves; and humans can know our good. All these assumptions can and should be challenged. And so, in our whirlwind tour of figures who come to stand in for vast cultural transformations, we come to someone who is less of a cultural hero (and no longer a scientific hero at all) than he once was: Sigmund Freud.

Freud, in the modern cultural imagination, taught us that we are not self-transparent rational individuals who can continue along the road to greater and greater social and cultural progress. Instead, we are mysterious to ourselves, at the mercy of forces, drives, and desires that we neither understand nor can bring ourselves to acknowledge. In other words, he taught us about the *unconscious.* From Freud, we learned that infants are already sexual beings, that domestic family life is driven by denied desires to kill the father and sleep with the mother, or be the mother and sleep with the father, that civilization depends on the capacity to channel our "lower" desires in "higher" directions (particularly the process of training that teaches children to defecate only in the toilet), and so on. I say "we learned," but of course many if not most of the details of the Freudian project are assumed by most to be thoroughly discredited on the level of individual psychology. (Freud is rightly taken by many in queer theory to illuminate larger cultural forces and sensibilities.) Crucially, Freud is one of the figures through whom cultural transformations that led away from all the assumptions associated with a dualistic anthropology took place. As Freud recognized, the person is indeed divided, but not between a rational, knowing, and knowable higher faculty and an irrational, unknowing, desiring lower faculty. Instead, the person is divided in such a way that one is divided against oneself *and* cannot know oneself. One cannot know one's "true" desires or one's "true" motives for acting. At the same time, one is always a sexual, desiring being in every way and at every moment—that's the nature of being an imaginative, bodied being. No relationships are fully outside the sexual and desire-driven.

Freud is a flashpoint in the developments that cause the late 20th and early 21st century to be, for us, the age of gender and sexuality. With the help of Freud and others, we come to see gender and sexuality as central, rather than peripheral or relatively unimportant, to our very development as persons. To become a human being means to become a sexed and gendered person, with a sexuality that is central to our authentic humanity and that, if "repressed" (a very Freudian word!), will express itself in one way or another, possibly damaging us in the process. Freud came at the endpoint of the rise and eventual cultural dominance of the science of sexuality—of the rise of science- and science-like language as a way of understanding human beings, the dominance of medical authorities in forming and classifying populations, and in that practice of classification depending in very basic ways on gender and sexuality as central categories.

In short, just like every other aspect of human self-understanding and social organization, gender and sexuality have a history—both as a history that varies over time and culture, and as a history that varies in the importance gender and sexuality are given in understanding the self. We can illustrate such changes in evaluation briefly. A very influential argument by Thomas Laqueur claims that over time, the West has shifted from a one-sex to a two-sex model. For Aristotle, or Aquinas, women were defective men—they had less bodily heat, and so were not a fundamentally different gender, but a less well developed example of a single gender. Only later are men and women understood as two fundamentally different sexes—an understanding that is now again being challenged from a very different direction, the reduction of sex and gender to two and only two alternatives.[6] Laqueur's argument is about the history of sex and gender across time and culture. This reflects historical variability in the *content* of sex and gender. In contrast, when on the first day of my queer theology class, I ask students to write down their legal names, degree programs, and year, as well as their preferred names and pronouns, this practice reflects the centrality of gender identity in cultural, legal, and theological struggles over the right ordering of human relationships. This reflects historical variability in the *importance and significance* of sex and gender.

Christians participate in all these struggles, on every side. Some argue that God intends two and only two sexes, oriented to each other for marriage and reproduction, so that biological sex determines the cultural forms of gender expression appropriate to each. Others argue very differently, in part on the basis of the cultural transformations we have just reviewed. In the next chapter, we turn our attention to those arguments.

6. See Laqueur, *Making Sex.*

# 2

# APOLOGETIC STRATEGIES

IN THIS CHAPTER, I rehearse apologetic strategies that queer theologians use to defend queer and trans* lives in order to make the case that queer theology is not about apologetics, or at least that it *should* not be about apologetics. Most Christians come to queer theology (if they do so at all!), looking for apologetic strategies. Given that many Christians argue that Christian sexual morality prohibits any sexual expression between persons of the same sex, and any genital sexual expression outside of marriage, and that some Christians argue that the sex assigned children at birth is God-ordained, and so denied only at the risk of damnation, the search for theological and biblical interpretive strategies for responding to such claims is understandable. Yet arguments on both sides of the case are often *ex post facto* (after the fact). The arguments one finds convincing are the arguments for the view one has come to have—for reasons other than argument! This can be seen in the many cases in which the mind of a Christian who condemns trans* or queer people is changed by encounter with a beloved trans* or queer other, such as a child or close friend. Perhaps one has believed that such persons are in rebellion against God, disdainful of God's revealed will. Instead, one comes to sympathize in their struggle. One might see that living openly, while not solving every or even most of the difficulties of human existence, still has good effects in the life of a loved one. And so, one might find one's previous evaluation of trans* or queer people shifting: rather than certainty and condemnation, one might ask oneself whether there are other ways to interpret the biblical texts that have come to be entrenched as "texts of terror"[1] to trans* and queer people.

Therefore, apologetic strategies can at a minimum be useful to those who worry that the arguments on the side of queer- and trans-affirming Christians are not as theologically rich as those on the other side; overall, it is likely that the reverse is the case. Some of these arguments will appeal more than others, depending on what considerations one finds decisive in theological matters in general. The categories offered here for grouping apologetic strategies should be taken only as a potentially illuminating organization, not as an exhaustive or absolute assignation of any particular author or argument to one category rather than another. The assessments of some of the arguments are my own; they are decidedly open to contestation, but I hope to make the basis of such assessments clear.

## IS GOD MALE?

Queer apologists argue that the implications of assuming that God prohibits same-sex relationships are disastrous

1. The expression is Phyllis Trible's.

for thinking about God's relationships to the world. Theologically speaking, one needs to defend or explain divine heterosexism somehow. That is, if one assumes that God prohibits homosexuality, why does God do so? Presumably, there's a divinely intended meaning that lies in heterosexuality. At the heart of the most sophisticated arguments against homosexuality lies Ephesians 5, which is read by some to imply that the theological meaning of gender and sexual differentiation in human existence is that relationships between men and women are images of, and point to, the relationship between Christ and the church.[2] Thus, human relationships must be heterosexual, for Christ is male and the church is the bride of Christ, and so symbolically female. Other than the argument from reproduction (which reduces sexual and erotic relationality to the aim only of making children, neglecting the many other blessings of sexuality in human existence), this is the only *positive* argument that can ultimately be given for holding exclusive heterosexuality as the only divinely sanctioned sexuality. But it is an argument that, very quickly, brings with it a host of other consequences—most importantly, the implication that maleness represents God in a way that femaleness never does.

There are several different ways to make this point. While scholars have worked hard to find female or feminine representations of God in the Bible, it is not that easy to do so, beyond images of divine tenderness, God's maternal care for creation, and the influence of Lady Wisdom on Christology.[3] Yahweh is sometimes represented as a jealous husband to an unfaithful, whorish Israel. Much of the Bible presumes that women's sexuality belongs to men. Even the

2. See Kerr, *Twentieth-Century Catholic Theologians*.

3. In the chapter on Marcella Althaus-Reid, we'll think further about whether we should seek *representation* or *transformation*.

Ten Commandments share that assumption ("You shall not covet your neighbor's wife," listed equally with his house and cattle; when I was a child, I interpreted this as showing that Moses didn't remember the original, divinely-written Ten Commandments with perfect accuracy, since obviously God would not have directed the commandments only at men).

In Christian traditions of symbolic or typological interpretation, in which events before the coming of Christ are later interpreted as indications or precursors of events fulfilled in Christ, Eve's creation from Adam's side prefigures the birth of the church from the side of Christ. (We'll encounter the church's birth from Christ's side again shortly.) But in neither Christ's nor Adam's case is gender equality necessarily implied. Christianity has been heavily patriarchal, valuing men more highly than women and, in practical terms, assigning a God-representing function to men that women never inhabit. Those who want to defend exclusive heterosexuality often try to respond with a claim of functional subordination without ontological inequality. That's a fancy way of claiming that God intends women to be subordinate to men without being unequal to them: different but equal. God initiates, leads, and decides, and the (feminine) church, made up of men and women, responds, receives, and obeys. In order to represent that difference within creation, men play the role of God in relation to women. So men initiate, lead, and decide, and women respond, receive, and obey. Now, for many of us, the idea that such a form of relationship is one of equality is just absurd. But there are other theological problems that result. By valuing men over women and associating men with God, God is reduced to an idol. One way or another, God's direct (rather than mediated) relation to all creation and God's transcendence of all creation both disappear.[4]

## ARGUMENTS FROM HISTORICAL DISTANCE

In the introduction, we briefly rehearsed some of the ways in which sex, gender, and sexuality have a history. A variety of apologetic strategies build on that fact to say that the expressions of same-sex eroticism that appear to be condemned in scripture are not actually discussing what we know now as homosexuality or queerness. Leviticus, for instance, is concerned about upholding boundaries between pure and impure in general, and draws those lines in places that are generally unfamiliar or unconvincing to most of us. Mixing cotton and linen doesn't worry us, so why should lying with a man as if with a woman bother us? The same general principle regarding the importance of purity and the threat of pollution[5] underlies both worries; thus if one is disregarded, the other may be also. Is the *land* defiled by eating impure animals, as the Leviticus code assumes? As Saul Olyan argues on philological grounds, the condemned act is that of the "active" partner in male-male anal intercourse. No other sexual acts between men, and no sexual acts between women, are condemned at all.[6]

Levitical codes worry about boundary transgression: things that don't clearly belong to one category or another are generally forbidden. But Levitical codes are also written within a patriarchal context in which women (and women's sexuality) are assumed to belong to men, rape can lead to marriage, and giving birth renders a woman unclean. For

4. Tanner, *Politics of God*; and Tonstad, *God and Difference*.

5. Douglas, "Abominations of Leviticus," in *Purity and Danger*, 51–71.

6. Olyan, "And with a Male You Shall Not Lie."

a boy, she is unclean for a week, for a girl, for two weeks, and in both cases she has to render both a burnt offering and a sin offering (Leviticus 12). As in many surrounding cultures—and this has not necessarily changed much in the interim!—one of the reasons sexual relations between men might be worrisome was that feminization of any kind is taken to dishonor men. Being like a woman, or allowing oneself to be treated like a woman, suggests that one is not enough of a man. Forbidding sex between men is not, then, really about sex between men, but about maintaining the boundaries of masculinity, just like making women unclean for two weeks rather than one after giving birth to a girl is a religious and cultural way to maintain the greater value of boys over girls.

There are several texts in the New Testament that many interpret in similar ways. First Cor 6:9–10 lists a number of people who will not inherit the kingdom of God, including the greedy, the drunk, and *malakoi oude arsenokoitai*. In 1 Tim 1:9–10, we learn that the law came for the sinful, "homosexuals" (in some translations; *arsenokoitais* originally), those who break promises, and others who disdain the gospel entrusted to the pseudonymous Pauline author. The literature on the meaning of both Greek terms is vast, especially since *arsenokoitai* is a so-called *hapax legomenon*, a word that appears only once in the Bible (although it appears in both places, the assumption among most scholars is that the 1 Timothy list is a citation of the authentically Pauline 1 Corinthians appearance). The apologist will typically point out that the notion we currently have, of homosexuality as an inborn, unchanging, lifelong orientation exclusively toward one sex did not exist in the Greco-Roman, or Jewish, thought-worlds within which Paul was writing. To varying degrees at various times, both Roman and especially Greek culture had no real difficulty with the idea that a virile, masculine man, maybe in his early 20s, might desire a boy/young man around the age of 16–18, and might mentor him sexually and intellectually. The "active," "insertive" partner did nothing to compromise his masculinity, although the "passive," penetrated partner was somewhat disdained, and sexual activity outside those boundaries (with older men or younger boys) would have been despised.[7] Thus, what may be in view here is temple prostitution, older men refusing to cease chasing adolescents, adolescents refusing to give up homosexual relations even as they got older and lost the storied attractiveness of youth just before the beard comes in fully, or even, in one of the more creative (but in some ways quite plausible) interpretations, about straight men having sex with other men.

Since no conception of homosexuality as an orientation, or even of *sexuality* as a person-constituting aspect of human existence, would have existed for either Paul or his pseudonymous imitator, he simply *cannot* be thinking about sex between gay men, since such a concept doesn't exist in his context. Thus, if he was thinking of sex between men, it would have been between men effectively considered straight (even though neither concept, straight or gay, existed for Paul). *Malakoi* also has connotations of softness, weakness, or femininity, so again it may be that gender, not sexuality, is what is at stake.[8]

At least one other argument that combines historical distance with other theological concerns should be mentioned: the argument from the analogy with slavery. On the textual level, the Bible has no difficulty with slavery as such. Several parallel New Testament texts instruct slaves who are followers of Christ to obey their earthly masters as they would obey Christ, or for the sake of their faithfulness to

7. Halperin, *One Hundred Years*.
8. Martin, *Sex and the Single Savior*.

God (Eph 6:5; Col 3:22). Legal codes in the Hebrew Bible regulate slavery, and are concerned to avoid the permanent enslavement of Israelites, but slavery as such is not a problem for them. A variety of just-so stories in the Bible explain how this nation came to be enslaved, or how this other group of people was rightly slaughtered. Slavery plays a significant role in the genesis of all three monotheistic religions, via Abraham's slave-concubine-wife Hagar, who gave birth to Ishmael.

Thus, when abolitionists needed to reinterpret biblical texts to support ending slavery, it was no easy task that they undertook. They had to center some biblical narratives over others. God's liberation of the Israelites from Egypt became a central interpretive lens for understanding and contextualizing other scriptural texts. Similarly, apologetic arguments regarding sexuality typically center Gen 1:26–27 and Gal 3:28 to suggest that all people are equally created in the image of God. The distinction between male and female doesn't matter Christianly, following baptism, and persons who are queer, trans*, intersex, and nonbinary should accept and celebrate that God created them that way. A strong case can be made that if one knows slavery to be wrong, and believes that one's Christian commitments reflect that knowledge, one has already come to interpret scripture in the way one must in order to recognize that the distinction between heterosexuality and homosexuality is theologically unimportant or unjustified. Generally, people don't need to give all kinds of reasons why slavery is wrong, nor do they spend any time wrestling with the biblical passages that endorse slavery. Similarly, once one recognizes that there are no good reasons to believe that it's wrong to be gay, trans*, intersex, queer, or nonbinary, one doesn't need to keep coming up with arguments dealing with the biblical passages that some interpret differently. Instead, one can get on with other issues.

## ARGUMENTS FROM REPRESENTATION AND REINTERPRETATION

The search for ancestors and antecedents is often important to queer, trans*, and genderqueer or nonbinary people. Finding antecedents in biblical and Christian symbolic histories can reassure queer, trans*, and nonbinary people that what Nancy Wilson calls "our tribe"[9] has always been part of the history of the people of God. The examples of David and Jonathan and Ruth and Naomi, sometimes even Jesus and John the Beloved Disciple, are especially popular with gay men and lesbians. David loved Jonathan with a love surpassing the love of women, and David was loved and chosen by God. Ruth swears an oath to Naomi that where Naomi goes, Ruth will follow, thus creating at least an antecedent for a vowed lesbian relationship, some think. Jesus' most intimate relationship was with another man, the man whom Jesus loved.

Trans*, intersex, and genderqueer people sometimes find ancestors in other places: eunuchs, particularly the ones from Jeremiah, Acts, and Matthew, and the tradition of Christian symbolic interpretation that finds the womb from which the church is born in the spear-wound in Jesus' side. Eunuchs, in the ancient world, included a wide variety of people that now might be categorized as trans*, intersex, genderqueer, or nonbinary,[10] so their presence in

9. Wilson, *Our Tribe.*

10. There's no transhistorical continuity in matters of gender, but an analogy can be drawn between different ways of organizing and troubling a sex-gender system in various cultural and historical contexts. For different approaches to the relationship between persons

several biblical passages is quite significant. In Jeremiah 38, Ebed-melech, an Ethiopian eunuch, appeals to the king on the prophet Jeremiah's behalf. Jeremiah has been falsely accused of deserting to the side of the Babylonians when he tries to leave Jerusalem to receive his share of family property elsewhere. He has been deposited in a well where he is likely to starve to death. Ebed-melech tells the king that Jeremiah is being treated unjustly, and is given permission to save him from starvation. Sensitive to the pain Jeremiah is in after a period of mistreatment, he knows that the ropes he will need to use to pull Jeremiah out will hurt him, so he finds old clothes and rags and tells Jeremiah to put them under his armpits to protect himself from the ropes. Perhaps as a result of this kind act, Ebed-melech is given his own personal promise through Jeremiah that he will survive the fall of Jerusalem (Jeremiah 39:15–18). Importantly, Ebed-melech is presented both as an instrument through which God's will is fulfilled, and as someone for whom God has such care that he, quite unusually, is given his own word of prophecy and protection.

In Acts 8, an angel of the lord tells the apostle Philip to travel out of Jerusalem along the road to Gaza. Along the way, he comes across an Ethiopian eunuch, the treasurer of the queen of the Ethiopians, who is returning from worshipping in Jerusalem. Like other Gentiles, the eunuch was restricted to worshipping in the outer court of the temple. As he travels, he is seated in his chariot reading the book of Isaiah. Upon further explicit instructions from the Spirit, Philip goes up to him to ask him whether he understands

with intersex conditions and eunuchs, see Joseph A. Marchal, "Who Are You Calling a Eunuch?! Staging Conversations and Connections between Feminist and Queer Biblical Studies and Intersex Advocacy," 29–54, and Megan K. DeFranza, "Virtuous Eunuchs: Troubling Conservative and Queer Readings of Intersex and the Bible," 55–77, both in Cornwall, *Intersex, Theology, and the Bible.*

what he is reading. The eunuch asks for help in interpretation, and Philip explains to him that the words he is reading, about a lamb led to slaughter (Isa 53:7–8), refer to Jesus. They are still traveling in the Ethiopian's chariot when they pass some water, so the Ethiopian asks to be baptized. After the baptism, the Spirit takes Philip away, and the eunuch "went on his way rejoicing" (Acts 8:39, NRSV). The eunuch is thus among those added to the believers in Jesus in the very early days following the descent of the Holy Spirit at Pentecost, and one of few sought out by direct divine instruction and intervention—before even the conversion of Saul into Paul. He is perhaps the first Gentile convert to the way of Jesus. Based on this story, it is simply absurd to have debates about whether trans* and gender-nonconforming people can be included in the church. They've been in the church all along! *God* made that happen. In an enigmatic saying in Matt 19:12, Jesus distinguishes between those born eunuchs, those made eunuchs by others, and those become eunuchs "for the sake of the kingdom of heaven" (NRSV) which, at a minimum, suggests that gender or genital transformation (however one wishes to understand the results of gender confirmation surgery) is permissible— and might even be undertaken for God's sake.[11]

Those who undergo gender confirmation surgery also sometimes find great meaning in a long history of interpreting the side-hole as a womb.[12] The crucified Jesus' side is pierced by a Roman soldier's spear. Out flow blood and water, and out of that side hole, the church is born. The interpretation of the wound in Jesus' side as a kind of womb is an old one. It reached what may have been its apotheosis in

11. For an important critique of these strategies, see Marcia McMahon, "Trans Liberating Feminist and Queer Theologies," in Beardsley and O'Brien, eds., *This Is My Body*, 65–66.

12. Partridge, "Side Wound, Virgin Birth, Transfiguration."

Hernnhut in Germany in the 1740s, when devotion to the side hole was at the heart of Moravian piety. Hymns sung to the side hole included lines like "Charming hole of mine, I . . . give you, my darling, Thousands of smacking kisses . . . Hold your little mouth to me, Kissing, kissing must be done. . . . Deep inside, just deep inside, Yes deep, real deep, therein, Whoever wants to be blessed."[13] Little reinterpretation is required to see the symbolic morphology in play, but visual representations of the side hole clarify what little ambiguity there may be, as they are more vulva-like than even a Georgia O'Keefe flower. Jesus' own body thus bears the marks of multiple ways of inhabiting gender.

## JESUS WAS GOOD, PAUL WAS BAD

The heading of this section is playful, but not too inaccurate regarding one of the most popular apologetic strategies. After all, Jesus said to the woman caught in adultery: "Neither do I condemn you. Go your way, and from now on do not sin again" (John 8:11, NRSV). He sat with the woman at the well, mostly unworried about her complicated sexual and romantic history. Jesus had close, affectionate relationships with men and women (including Mary, Mary, and Martha) and lived off the financial resources of some wealthy women (Luke 8). Jesus was about radical inclusion, many argue, dissolving all boundaries in the establishment of a kingdom that privileged tax collectors and sex workers over rigid, prissy Pharisees (just like Paul was!). Paul, on the other hand, was sex-negative, misogynistic, and terrified of the rightly ordered body of Christ dissolving into chaos if women were allowed to speak, much less prophesy. Sure, in Gal 3:28 he recognizes that the consequence of the gospel he preaches is that all these binary divisions (between Jew and

13. Vogt, "'Honor to the Side,'" 92.

Greek, slave and free, and male and female) are dissolved in Christ, but he wasn't able to recognize the implications of his own insight, and so maintained that women must cover their hair and should not preach freely. And, devastatingly, Paul's anti-body, anti-erotic, boundary-maintaining worries came to mark Christianity for centuries, distorting the central implications of Jesus' radical message of inclusion and acceptance.

There are numerous theological, textual, and interpretive worries that accompany this strategy. Here, I will name only two. First, there is no Christianity without Paul. Several of Paul's letters are the oldest books in the New Testament. Paul, the apostle to the Gentiles, is in a sense the one who includes every Christian not of Jewish descent into the community that follows Christ (although we should not forget the Ethiopian eunuch). Contrasting Paul with Jesus in this way also ignores some rather complicated moments in Jesus' ministry, in particular his response to the Syro-Phoenecian woman who requested healing for her daughter, and was told, "It is not fair to take the children's food and throw it to the dogs" (Mark 7:27, NRSV; also in Matt 15:26). Jesus relents when the woman accepts his designation of her and her daughter as dogs and cleverly turns it against Jesus, but this is not necessarily a Jesus who practices radical acceptance of all equally. Jesus did come to heal the sick and set the captives free, and many Christians believe that his ministry extends to all creation. But Jesus may only have come to that insight himself over time.

Searching for a non-Pauline Christianity also participates in a long and ugly Christian history of seeking to excise and deny the Jewish elements and antecedents of Christianity. Through much of Christian history, both the Gospels and Paul's writings were taken to represent a Christian condemnation of Judaism for its legalistic and moralistic characteristics, in contrast to Christianity's message of grace and freedom. Extensive and brutal Christian persecution of Jews was justified along just these lines. Such persecution includes the creation of ghettos, pogroms, and, as the culmination of a cultural and theological logic at the heart of Europe and the West's Christian legacy, the Holocaust. But Jesus, like Paul, was Jewish. In recent decades, scholars have helped to clarify the degree to which many early Christian conflicts, or conflicts between "Jews" and "Christians," the traces of which we find in New Testament writings, were actually intra-Jewish conflicts, conflicts between Jews who believed in Jesus and Jews who did not. Both distinguishing between Jesus and Paul, and distinguishing between Jesus and his (Jewish) context, on the basis of the difference between freedom and law, or law and grace, participates in the perpetuation of these anti-Semitic interpretive strategies.

## GAYS AREN'T SINNERS

Some apologetic strategies focus on what we might call the "gay is good" case. Romans 1:26–7 suggests that when men and women exchange proper intercourse with persons of the other gender for the same, it is a punishment for sin that leads to any number of other sins, including murder. In 1 Cor 6 and 1 Tim 1, the apparent condemnation takes place within a long list of sins as well. But queer relationships aren't like that, some apologists argue. Many of them are faithful, loving, committed relationships of mutual care and self-sacrifice. And queer people aren't murderous promise-breakers; they are loving people with high moral standards—maybe even higher moral standards than people in general have. Thus, the authors of these biblical texts are just wrong about homosexuality. The fruits of the Spirit are peace, gentleness, long-suffering, and those *are* the characteristics of many queer relationships, as can be seen in the networks of fictive kinship that queer people rejected by their families create and in the way gays and lesbians came together to care for the gay men afflicted by the AIDS crisis. Even the patience of queer people with the slowness of Christian churches to include them fully exhibits the true Christian witness of queers.

While there's no reason to believe that queer people are more sinful than others, there are reasons to worry about this strategy as well. All persons *are*, I believe, sinners. Arguing that gays *aren't* may participate in the production of hierarchies of sinners, where some people are only sort of sinners (but really good) and others are really sinners (so really bad). That, as we'll see in later chapters, is an anti-queer and, in my view, theologically unjustifiable practice. Yet condemnations of queer people assume that queers are deviant and ethically misguided at a fundamental level.

Gays aren't sinners is sometimes connected with another, more casual set of assumptions. Some assume that queers are born this way and they can't help it. But God creates all people good; God has created them this way; therefore, they ought to love and affirm themselves in the way God made them. On one level, there's nothing wrong with this argument. It's one that is often made from a pastoral direction to those who have experienced condemnation of what they experience as their inner being and truest reality. God *does* call creation good, and God does love all of God's creation.

There are some reasons to be cautious of this strategy, however. For one thing, it participates in two assumptions that many queer theorists would question: that gender and sexuality are the most authentic inwardness of a human being, and that sexuality, like gender, is born, not made.

(We'll return to questions like this in the next chapter.) In Simone de Beauvoir's famous words, "One is not born, but rather becomes, a woman." This means that gender is not an unchanging characteristic of inwardness, of our deepest identities. One learns how to be a woman, and much of that learning participates in systems of domination. One is told that girls behave like this and boys like this, and significant aspects of one's life are organized according to gender (hence the absurd panic advanced by some about whether trans* people should be allowed to use the bathroom that conforms to their gender). Gender is one of the places where injustice is lived. Whether the solution to gender's entrenchment in injustice requires gender justice, the end of gender, or both, is an argument we'll return to later. For now, we should simply ask ourselves whether the born-this-way argument 1) can include those who don't feel that they were born this way, but who live nonnormative sexualities and gender identities; 2) requires that every person have a God-willed gender; 3) requires divine investment in a binary gender system (to account for those who experience themselves as exclusively homosexual or heterosexual).

## GOD'S LOVE RADICALLY TRANSGRESSES EVERY BOUNDARY

At the heart of many queer apologetic strategies lies the claim beautifully summed up in the title of Patrick Cheng's *Radical Love*. Christianity is about a message of radical, boundary-destroying love. Christianity, rightly understood, is about the transgression of boundaries. Christians believe in a God whose love undoes every binary.

What is a binary, you ask? Good question! Binaries are organizing categories of social existence in many cultural contexts. Binaries divide reality into categories of this-or-that, or this-not-that. Examples of binaries many in the West are familiar with include male/female, nature/culture, true/false, light/dark, and so on. Many cultural theorists believe binaries to be at the heart of many of the hierarchies that organize and stratify social and cultural life. Typically, one term in a binary is valued more highly than the other term, and the more highly valued terms are associated with each other. So male is associated with culture, with reason, with light, and so on, and female is associated with nature, falseness, darkness, and so on.

Following influential thinkers like Jacques Derrida and Judith Butler, who show that the valued term in a binary actually depends on its opposite, and that binaries contradict themselves internally, many queer apologists argue that the destruction, or transgression, of binaries is central to the Christian message. Again, Gal 3:28 appears at the heart of such strategies: Jew/Greek, slave/free, and male/female are all examples of binaries that, Paul claims, no longer hold for those who are in Christ. Jesus also transgresses the boundary between life and death, as he is crucified but resurrected, and the boundary between God and human, as he is both God and human. Heterosexual/homosexual belongs to the list of binaries destroyed or transgressed by Christianity, the argument runs, following the Christian irrelevance of the distinction between male and female. Christianity is at its heart a radical, boundary-transgressing message of God's love, which includes all without distinction. Christianity is about the end of the distinction between insider and outsider; all are welcome.

Many of these arguments hinge on two particular assumptions about Christ. First, these arguments claim that Christ "transgresses" the boundary between divine and human. Some theologians even say that Christ transgresses the binary between God and creation. But in the main lines of historical Christian interpretation, there are reasons to be wary of such claims. The Chalcedonian definition, which was proclaimed in 451, is of the most influential statements of the rules by which Christians speak about Christ. It says that Jesus is fully divine and fully human "without confusion, without division, without separation," both in both, not a *tertium quid* (third thing). Jesus is not, then, a hybrid of divine and human that would be neither divine nor human. Jesus is *both* divine and human.

For most Christian theologians, this surprising, unimaginably intimate union between divinity and humanity is possible because God is infinite. God's infinity means that God is not a being among other beings or a thing among other things—indeed, in a certain sense God is not *a* being at all.

Beings and things are distinguished from each other by their differences from each other, and so are understood and defined in relation to each other. But if God were distinguished from creation by creation's differences from God, then God would be whatever creation is not. Such a God would not be infinite, but would be bounded by creation as God's contrast. Instead, the main lines of historical Christian interpretation argue that God is beyond both similarity and difference with respect to creation—God is the difference beyond difference. That means too that there is not as such a "boundary" between divine and human, and certainly divine and human are not a binary. It's because God is God—transcendent—that God can be united with creation, with humanity, in Christ without either violating creaturely existence or giving up God's divinity.

Second, these arguments hinge on the several ways in which Christ's body is symbolically multigendered. The church is the body of Christ. The church is, of course, made up of people of many different genders and none (people who are agender). Thus, Christ's body is multigendered. To make the point another way: as we've seen, Christians have a long history of understanding the spear-wound in Christ's side on the cross as a symbolic womb out of which the church is born. Christ's body is then both morphologically male (in that he was circumcised) and morphologically female, or at least maternal, in that he has a womb. As the scene with Thomas in the upper room suggests, Christ's glorified body retains its wounds. For some trans* people, whose bodies bear marks of transformation, Christ's glorified body meaningfully confirms the divine value of their bodies.

Important though these insights are, some difficulties remain. Although Christ's body is made up of people of all genders and none, Christ remains the head of the church—that's the sense in which the church is his body. The image depends on a hierarchical relationship between Christ, the head, and the church, which belongs to him. It's difficult, then, to use the image to dislodge his masculinity, especially because both his masculinity and femininity become *symbolic*. That's mostly different from how gender is encountered in lives. In our lives, we are and we encounter people of many different genders and none. That's how we experience gender: in our bodies and in our relations with others. We don't usually encounter the genital morphology of people we are not sexually intimate with—and in any case, genital morphology doesn't determine gender. Instead, gender presentation takes place through self-identification as well as a variety of culturally coded symbols and behaviors, symbols and behaviors that we learn in our bodied relations.

But our relationship with Christ is different. It is, in a real way, an *imagined* relation. (This does not mean that it is an *imaginary* relation.) That is, our understanding of

Christ's gender is mediated through stories (in which his surroundings seem to experience him as male) and through mental, theological, and literal pictures. Representing gender symbolically depends on assumptions about the fit between the genital morphology that is symbolized, and the gender that symbology indicates. Put more straightforwardly, some people who have wombs aren't women, and some women don't have wombs. But representing the spear-wound in Christ's side as a womb that therefore renders Christ feminine or maternal requires representing femininity or maternity through a womb, the very kind of identification between a particular bodily morphology and a gender that many queer and trans* people contest. For some, such an identification may be important and meaningful, while others may find it troubling.

## THE ARGUMENT FROM FOOD AND CIRCUMCISION

The argument from food and circumcision is both theologically and theoretically insightful, and quite plausible on scriptural grounds. Many of the conflicts in the early days of the movement of Jesus-followers that would become Christianity, particularly as recorded in Paul's writings and the book of Acts, were about issues of food and circumcision. Must followers of Christ be circumcised? Must they abstain from food offered to idols? Must they abstain from unclean foods? Must Jewish followers of Christ abstain from eating with Gentiles? As we saw, in Leviticus, many of the fundamental organizing categories are about what can licitly be eaten, and what cannot. Worries about food are also worries about bodily boundaries and their transgression, fear of bodily pollution, and so on.

Circumcision, for example, is a bodily (and gendered) marker of belonging, signifying that one is an heir of the covenant made with Abraham. Since inclusion into that covenant is a condition of salvation, ought not new believers in Jesus also to be circumcised? Paul, frustrated at these debates, exclaims, "Neither circumcision nor uncircumcision counts for anything, the only thing that counts is faith working through love" (Gal 5:6, NRSV). "For neither circumcision nor uncircumcision is anything; but a new creation is everything!" (Gal 6:15, NRSV). "There is no longer Greek and Jew, circumcised and uncircumcised, barbarian, Scythian, slave, and free; but Christ is all and in all!" (Col 3:11, NRSV). Circumcision is good and valuable, especially if it expresses the inward as well as the outward being of the person. But circumcision is not itself the point anymore. Insisting that Gentile believers in Christ be circumcised is an irrelevant distraction. What matters is faith working through love.

The analogy between food and sex runs throughout much of the biblical text. Peter, hungry and praying on the roof of Cornelius' house (Acts 10), is told to rise and eat of food he *knows* to be unclean, violating what he rightly recognizes as explicit divine command *not* to eat of these foods. In Galatians 2, Paul rebukes Cephas (quite possibly the apostle Peter), who, having eaten with the Gentiles until the rest of the delegation from Jerusalem arrives, stops eating with them to Paul's scorn. Paul suggests that in so doing, Peter is denying the gospel. Despite extensive biblical concern with what should be eaten, in what way, and with whom (a far greater proportion of the biblical text deals with food than with sex), Christians tend to see food practices as "matters that can safely be left either to individual choice or respectful dialogue,"[14] while many think sexuality is at the heart of Christian identity and faithfulness.

But even Paul spends more time discussing food practices than he does matters of sexual behavior. Both food and circumcision lie at the heart of dividing lines between religious insider and outsider in the biblical text. Paul is quite clear in Romans 9–11 that salvation for believers in Jesus, whether such believers are Jews or Gentiles, comes through the line of inheritance from Abraham. God's covenant with Abraham has not been suspended, Paul thinks: rather, it is in the process of being fulfilled. Gentile Christians should be grateful that its fulfillment has been delayed long enough for them to be included, by God's gracious mercy.

What one eats, when, and with whom; how one's morphologically male body is marked religiously: for Paul, these questions are at least as fundamental as questions of sexual behavior. But now, the dividing line no longer runs between those who follow divine food regulations and those who don't, or those who are circumcised, and those who aren't. *In Christ, there is full liberty.* (Care must again be taken here to avoid a structure of argument that can be turned to anti-Semitic or anti-Jewish use. Paul is a Jew making an argument grounded in the Palestinian Judaism of his day.)[15]

That liberty must not be used to cause one's siblings to stumble, however. The stronger in faith must avoid placing obstacles at the feet of those weaker in faith. And now we get to one of those wonderful inversions that Paul's arguments

14. Stone, *Practicing Safer Texts*, 5.

15. E. P. Sanders states directly that "on grace and works there is in fact agreement" between Paul and Palestinian Judaism, *Paul and Palestinian Judaism*, 548. For more on the risks of anti-Semitism in queer theology, see Tonstad, "Limits of Inclusion: Queer Theology and Its Others," 2–5, 14–17.

so often invite, because we can read Paul's distinction either way. Are heterosexual Christians the stronger in faith? Then they must avoid causing their weaker, queer siblings to stumble by placing obstacles in their way—presumably, by insisting that queer people reach a standard of sexual behavior (celibacy) that heterosexual Christians themselves do not meet. Are queer Christians the stronger in faith, since they recognize that all is clean? Then they must allow their heterosexual siblings to restrict their own practices as they choose. Queer Christians must not lure their heterosexual siblings into participating queer sexual practices. Romans 14 makes clear that while Paul believes that "everything is indeed clean" (v. 20, NRSV), if someone believes that something is unclean, then it is, *for that person*. So one must not look down on that person on those grounds. At the same time, one cannot impose one's own restrictions on others. "The faith that you have, have as your own conviction before God" (v. 22, NRSV). One condemns oneself if one does what one doubts is right, not if one follows one's convictions (v. 23).

It is, by the way, my own view that the implication of this argument is not only that the distinction between heterosexual and homosexual sexual practices no longer holds (although I do think that implication is valid). The implication of the argument is also that Christians should stop arguing over issues of sexual morality altogether, and instead should allow the discernment of the individual conscience before God to rule. Which is one of the theological reasons queer theology ought not to be about apologetics at all.

## THE ARGUMENT BEYOND NATURE

In excess of nature: *para physin* (rather than *kata physin*, according to nature). This Stoic language, used by Paul in

Romans, is at the heart of Eugene F. Rogers's apologetic argument in *Sexuality and the Christian Body: Their Way into the Triune God*. Scholars have come to recognize that rather than arguing that Christians supplanted Jews in the Abrahamic covenant, Paul in Romans 9–11 actually argues that Christians are *grafted onto* the Jewish covenantal tree— that is, Gentile Christians are included into the everlasting covenant God established with Abraham.[16] In *excess* of nature, *against* nature, God grafts Gentiles onto the Jewish olive tree.

But the attentive reader of Romans has heard that language before: in Romans 1, describing the excess of or contrariety to nature characteristic of the desire of men for men and women for women. Aha! We have encountered another Pauline reversal. Rogers identifies two of the crucial elements of his argument as "God's acting 'contrary to' or 'beyond' nature in incorporating the Gentiles into the Jewish olive tree (Rom. 11:24) [and] God's predilection for irregular sexuality in salvation history, as in the cases of the women named in the genealogy of Jesus."[17]

Gentile Christians deny God's action beyond or against nature to their peril, since it is only on that condition that they themselves get into the divine covenant at all. Matthew's genealogy of Jesus includes Tamar, who dressed up like a sex worker in order to get pregnant by her father-in-law, Judah; Rahab, a Canaanite sex worker; Ruth, a Moabite woman (so, in biblical logic, descended from the sexual intercourse or rape of a drunken and insensible Lot by his older daughter); and the unnamed Bathsheba, Uriah's wife stolen by king David after he spied on (stalked?) her bathing. To intensify the surprise of this genealogy, it is in fact a genealogy of *Joseph*, who is *not* (according to Matthew)

16. Stowers, *Romans*.
17. Rogers, *Sexuality and the Christian Body*, 3.

the father of Jesus, but the husband of Jesus' mother. Thus, sex work, rape, incest, murder (which is what David did to Uriah, in practice), and adoption are all part of the lineage through which God brings Godself into the world in a new way in Jesus.

Now, one may have some reservations about using analogies to incest, rape, and murder to justify homosexuality on Christian grounds. Rogers's argument is a conservative argument for the recognition of same-sex marriages as a path to sanctification for gay people, just like marriage is a path to sanctification for straight people, not an argument that goes beyond (somewhat reluctant) recognition of the validity of life-long, vowed, marital relationships between persons of the same sex. But Rogers is right to point to the many ways of being human and sexual in the world that God incorporates into God's salvific actions.

## THE ARGUMENT FROM ESCHATOLOGICAL TRANSFORMATION

What will we look like in heaven? We will still be bodied, for as we saw in the introduction, the resurrection of Christ entails irreversible embodiment as a condition of human existence. Christianity promises no escape from the body. The body is transformed, but it is never left behind. But will our bodies look like they do now? Will humans still be male and female? Early Christians disagreed on these matters, but were often quite happy to speculate. Jesus specified that in heaven there is neither marrying nor giving in marriage, so in that sense *something* quite significant changes. How far down do such changes go? Will we be like the angels, who don't have genitals? Augustine believed that we will all be the right size and age in heaven (about 30, perfectly formed). Reporting the speculations of some who thought that all will become male, Augustine conceded that being female was natural, not a defect, and so held that women would remain women in the resurrection.

Origen, most charming of theologians, speculated that bodily perfection would apply also to form, and what form is more perfect than a sphere? I laugh every time I try to imagine a heaven of spherical forms . . . rolling around? Maybe he was imagining something more like we envision our solar system! At the time of writing this book, Gregory of Nyssa is the most influential early Christian writer for queer theologians. He believed that eschatological transformation would mean the end of gender. Gender was a concession to the needs of reproduction; once those needs are past, the time of gender will be also. Some early Christian authors believed that Adam and Eve remained virgins as long as they were in the Garden of Eden (since their children were not born until afterward). If so, the curse following the fall ("your desire shall be for your husband, and he shall rule over you," Gen 3:16, NRSV) might effectively mean that lived or reproductive heterosexuality belongs only to the order of fallen creation.

The implication of these arguments is that gender can't have the centrality for Christians that arguments for exclusive heterosexuality require it to have. If eschatological transformation takes human beings beyond gender, in some sense, then God isn't that concerned with enforcing normative gender standards on us.

## THE ARGUMENT FROM APOCALYPSE

In one of those gloriously strange Pauline texts, he exhorts his readers: "I mean, brothers and sisters, the appointed time has grown short; from now on, let even those who have wives be as though they had none, and those who mourn as though they were not mourning, and those who rejoice as though they were not rejoicing, and those who buy as though they had no possessions, and those who deal with the world as though they had no dealings with it. For the present form of this world is passing away" (1 Cor 7:29–31, NRSV). The time is short, and the form of this world is passing away. From now on, the old distinctions no longer hold, Paul thinks.

The biblical scholar J. Louis Martyn discusses the "apocalyptic antinomies" found in Paul. First, many of the old antinomies—binaries, you might say—no longer hold. They belong to the old order, the order of a world that was. But *now*, that world is over. Those distinctions, once so crucial, no longer matter. "Galatians . . . is about the death of one world, and the advent of another. . . . [O]ne knows the old world to have died, because . . . its fundamental structures are gone."[18] According to this argument, both homosexuality and heterosexuality belong to the old order. They stand, equally, under judgment as forms of life that will not remain in new creation. Their power is already broken.

Paul instructs people in presumptively heterosexual relationships to live *as if not*, for heterosexuality belongs to the form of this world, and the time is short. Homosexuality, no differently from heterosexuality, organizes the world according to categories that, in the contrast between the old world and *new creation*! (Pauline new creation should probably always have an exclamation point attached), no longer have any power or relevance. Indeed, when Paul says that he wishes everyone were like him, but it is better to marry than to burn—wouldn't that concession apply to people who aren't straight as much as to those who are? I should perhaps mention that I owe this apocalyptic application to

18. Martyn, "Apocalyptic Antinomies," 117–18.

sexuality to my father, Sigve K. Tonstad, who hopes for the renewal of this world and of all creation.

## THE ARGUMENT FROM JESUS' WORDS

Jesus, who as we saw above, sometimes seemed not to be too worried about sexual morality, also said: "Everyone who looks at a woman with lust, has already committed adultery with her in his heart" (Matt 5:28, NRSV). Most Christian condemnations of homosexuality turn on the distinction between an inclination and an act. Homosexual *inclinations* aren't sinful unless they are, shall we say, enacted. After the failure of ex-gay ministries like Exodus to turn gay Christians straight, and in order not to sound too judgmental in a world that has seen enough of the consequences of Christian judgment, many Western Christian churches (and even arguably the Roman Catholic church, during the papacy of Francis) depend heavily on distinguishing the inclination or temptation from the act.

This is the official public relations line of many of the churches that continue to condemn homosexuality. We don't condemn homosexual *people*, they aver, only homosexual *acts*. Given the cultural legitimacy that churches continue to lose on the basis of their homophobia and sexism, it's understandable that they would seek ways to moderate the intensity of their condemnation. Such churches, or those who have chosen to live celibate Christian lives because they are gay, argue that faithful gay celibacy will be rewarded in heaven, and constitutes a form of Christian friendship approved by God—as long as such friendship does not turn sexual. Homosexuals, like alcoholics, are given a difficult burden to bear from birth, but God will also give the power to overcome the inclination, or at least to avoid succumbing to it.

But such claims turn on a sharp disjunction between inclination and act that Jesus explicitly denies—at least for heterosexual men. If we take Jesus' words seriously, sexual sin doesn't necessarily have anything to do with what the body actually does, but lies in desire itself. Is Jesus implying that only asexuals are free of sexual sin? Certainly the theological justification for distinguishing inclination and act vanishes in light of Jesus' words. Rather than trying to free themselves from cultural opprobrium by using nicer language about gay people, homophobic churches ought to have the courage of their convictions and admit that they do think homosexuality, the *inclination*, is sinful. Otherwise, their homophobia turns out not to be theologically serious, I would argue.

Of course, given the sense many have of being gay since birth, or not having a choice (not all LGBTQ people think about gender or sexuality this way), such an admission would require homophobic churches to say also that some humans are born sinful in a way that others are not. Which would be a problem, since for just those churches, actual sin requires choice, an active participation or affirmation of the will. One thus has to come up with a complicated and extremely implausible image of the human person in which some part of the self experiences lust, but some other part of the self does not consent to that experience of lust (remember that we're not talking about lustful *acts* at all). One must then say that only the part of the self that isn't experiencing the lust is one's real self. But who then had the experience of lust that moved the other part of the self to refuse consent to the lustful inclination? While many of us have experienced desires that we decide not to act on, or desires that we decide not to indulge, it's still *we* who are those within which those desires move.

Alternatively, churches invested in the distinction between the inclination and the act might have to admit that homosexuality and heterosexuality are equally sinful, so that the distinction between them is no longer where the boundaries of Christian sexual morality ought to be drawn.

## THE ARGUMENT AGAINST JUDGMENT

The argument against judgment is connected with the arguments from food and circumcision, the argument against nature, and with apocalyptic concerns, but it is not grounded only there. Returning to the text in Rom 1:26–27, which also offers the only clear(-ish) reference to sex between women in the Bible, we tarry with the intensity of condemnation that Paul offers. Not only are men having sex with men and women with women, they are also wicked, depraved, envious, evil gossipers who disobey their parents and show no mercy! (Textually, all these characteristics stand side by side.) How disgusting they are, we mutter. What wickedness! we say to ourselves, with a sense of satisfaction that we are not like that.

And then, perhaps, we keep reading. "Therefore you have no excuse, whoever you are, when you judge others; for in passing judgment on another you condemn yourself, because you, the judge, are doing the very same things" (Rom 2:1, NRSV). Wait, what? I don't do those things. I'm not a depraved, evil sinner who deserves death! I'm not proud, but I'm not like that! (Ahem.) The continuation of the text forces us to ask: is Romans 1 about the condemnation of homosexuality, or about the condemnation of *judgment*? Is it a text that tells us how to distinguish between good people, who love God and of whom God approves, or is it a text that tells us that we're all in the same boat, as Romans 3 so clearly suggests?

In my first book, *God and Difference*, I situated the argument against judgment or distinction in relation to two other biblical texts, Matt 13:24–29 and Matt 25:31–46. Matt 25 is the well-known story of the separation of the sheep and the goats on the day of judgment. The criterion of separation is how the least among these are treated, and Jesus specifies that those who visited the poor and fed the hungry had, in truth, done all this to him. Matt 13, meanwhile, tells of the wheat and the weeds that grow together in the master's field. Zealous servants seek to weed out the weeds, but the master tells them to wait until the day of judgment, when he will separate them himself. I take these two texts (and many others could be added: judge not that you not be judged, the splinter in the other's eye vs. the log in my own, and so on) to imply that judging the righteousness of another should be left only to God. It is not my duty to police the views or behavior of others.

Thus, even if Christians who condemn homosexuality were right, sifting the wheat (queer-condemning Christians) from the chaff (queer Christians and their straight allies) should be left by them to God, rather than made into a principle of denominational and congregational distinction. Paul's instruction that each should be certain in their own conscience suggests too that my energies should be directed to aligning *my* behavior with *my* conscience.

Paul does lay one further instruction on Christians who believe all foods to be clean: not to despise or look down on siblings who have not come to that insight. Thus, Christians who hold that homosexuality and trans* and nonbinary gender experiences are in no way contrary to the will of God are tasked with a heavy burden, for the derogatory and sometimes persecutory acts of queer-condemning Christians cry out to be named, catalogued, and condemned. However, Paul's instruction means that while queer- and trans*-condemning Christians may be resisted (when seeking to enforce their views by means of law, when trying to split denominations on issues of sexuality, and in the act of condemnation), they cannot be met in response with the same judgment that they utter. Judgment of their actions too must be left to God.

## THEOLOGICAL ASSESSMENT

I said at the beginning of this chapter that I will argue that queer theology is not, or should not be, about apologetics. Having canvassed these apologetic arguments, it may be clear why that is so. Very few of the arguments we've looked at so far are theologically rich, insightful, illuminating—except, perhaps, the nexus of the arguments from food, circumcision, and judgment, which give us reasons not to argue about sexuality rather than reasons to accept homosexuality. Many of the arguments depend on conditions that are peripheral to central Christian concerns, while others depend for their effectiveness primarily on gaining Christian sanction for same-sex relationships. Is that all the insight that emerges for Christianity from queer, trans*, and nonbinary lives?

Most fundamentally, many of these arguments ignore the ambiguities of human existence, the ways in which our lives and their consequences are neither transparent to us nor fully within our power to determine. Many of these arguments also reflect contemporary allergies to central Christian notions about sin and salvation. The idea that human lives are broken and malformed at a very basic level participates, for many, in a culture of shame and guilt that needs to be resisted rather than affirmed. In the next chapter, we'll turn our attention to some reasons for questioning every one of these assumptions.

# 3

# THEOLOGY, SEXUALITY, AND THE QUESTION OF QUEER

IF, AS I HAVE suggested, queer theology should not be about apologetics, what should it be about? Queer studies often operates with assumptions about gender and sexuality that are quite foreign to those outside the field. This chapter rehearses some of those assumptions—but laying them out is not an easy task.

On the first day of my queer theology seminar, we walk through the syllabus, discussing the different readings. I warn students that much of what we'll be reading will not be theology, but texts from an academic discipline known as queer theory. These texts are difficult, written in unfamiliar, complex language. The language is difficult enough that many unfamiliar with the field either mock or dismiss the texts in question because they are so hard to read, I explain. I warn the students that they will find the reading hard, and that they should not be discouraged by the difficulty. If they persist, they will learn to speak queer theory the same way they learn to speak theology or any other unfamiliar language: through repetition, seeing the way words are used, and translation. (A dictionary helps too!) A few weeks later, a succession of students appears in my office hours to complain that these texts are so hard, and that they're worried that they're the only person in the class who isn't understanding them. What should they do?

When I was 19, I took a college class on feminist philosophy in which we read Judith Butler's classic *Gender Trouble*. It was the most convoluted writing I had ever encountered. I only knew some of the authors she was engaging, and I certainly didn't know all the psychoanalytic vocabulary with which she worked. I remember this experience because the class was one of the most generative academic experiences of my life. But when I look at *Gender Trouble* now, I don't find it particularly difficult or unclear (at least not on the level of language!). The years I've spent reading and teaching the text allow it to make sense.

Reading queer theory requires patience and repetition, and if you're interested, I certainly encourage you to undertake the project. It's also a lot of fun! But in this chapter, I give a brief, ordinary-language overview of some of the major ways of thinking about gender, sexuality, and the formation of human personhood characteristic of queer theory, and consider the implications of these ways of thinking for theology.

There are several risks entailed in such a procedure, and it's just as well to get them out on the table at once. First, there's the risk of oversimplification and distortion. If I try to rewrite discourses that see it as part of their nature to require a specialized vocabulary in ordinary language, am I really reporting accurately what these ways of speaking mean? Quite simply, the answer is no. I will do my best, but there is unavoidably some loss involved. That's especially true because queer theory, and some forms of queer theology, assume the importance of a relationship between the form and the content of language. That is, rather than assuming that form or genre is unimportant to what and how language means, such ways of speaking assume that form and genre significantly determine what and how language means. So in changing the form or genre, I'm giving up at least some part of the capacity of that language to accomplish its effects.

Second, there's the risk of what some would see as colonization—either of Christian theology by non-theological discourse, or of queer theory by Christianity. Here we're also touching on a question that we'll return to at the very end of the book: if and to what extent Christianity really can be queer. Third, there's the unavoidable fact—not risk—of particularity and partiality. This book is not written as a neutral report on "the state of the question" regarding queerness and Christianity; like (in reality) all books, it makes a case for a particular way of viewing these relationships. I am a Christian theologian who works in queer theory as well. Many Christian theologians and many queer theorists believe that combination is impossible. Those who think such a combination *is* possible often disagree about how such a task should be undertaken. We've already rehearsed many of the apologetic arguments that some believe are central to queer theology, whereas I've suggested that apologetics is of little theological value. At the same time, much of my own work in theology is more doctrine-heavy than most queer theologians would prefer.

Because this chapter is intended to be as readable as possible, I will indicate the major figures associated with the viewpoints I'm describing, but I won't go into detail about every one of them or their particular contributions. Instead, I'll focus on general ways of thinking about or approaching problems, ways of thinking about human beings, relationships, sexuality, and gender, and then offering suggestions for further reading should one want to go deeper into the particular discussion.

## NATURE OR NURTURE?
## OR IS THAT THE WRONG QUESTION?

Common-sense approaches to sex and gender often make arguments purportedly based on biology or evolutionary history to explain why men and women are the way they (supposedly) are. "Why Women Love to Shop," an article confidently declares. "Men were the hunters in our ancestral cultures," while women "were the primary gatherers . . . so they feel a need to check every berry on the bush to make sure they're getting the best deal." The research proving the point was based on a survey of undergraduate students' agreement or disagreement with statements the researchers had decided were characteristic of hunting or gathering behavior.[1] Women are hormonally determined to care more about bonding than sex, many claim, while men are evolutionarily wired to want to get as many women pregnant as possible; hence male non-monogamy and female disinterest in sex. We're probably all familiar with these overgeneralizing, simplistic approaches to the complexity of how different people behave. Scientists tell us just-so stories, stories that explain to us how things came to be the

1. Dye, "Why Women Love to Shop." And some think research in the humanities lacks rigor!

way they are. These stories, of course, tend to confirm that the way things are is how they should be, the outcome of natural processes. It's not just disagreements about gender roles that tend to be adjudicated this way. The search for the so-called gay gene, and the justification of homosexuality through the prevalence or distribution of same-sex interactions in the animal kingdom, have long proceeded along similar lines.

Theorists of sex and gender have raised questions about a number of the assumptions on which these practices depend. Explanations of this kind assume that nature simply expresses itself in culture—that cultural organization can be accounted for by evolutionarily determined genetic and hormonal factors. If we can identify the factors, then we recognize the immutable, or at least very powerful, factors that determine the way men and women live. It's easy to show that such explanations underplay the force of cultural factors. In contexts where monogamous heterosexual marriage is a cultural norm, many, maybe even most men in fact conform to that norm. Does culture override the supposedly biological drive toward sex with as many women as possible? What about the vast cultural and historical variability of gender roles and sexual behavior? But for many theorists of sex and gender, what's most important is not to challenge specific claims or forms of justification produced by evolutionary biologists and psychologists. The most important, most interesting question is rather why we assign to them—to science in general—the task of determining what is *really* the case about gender.

The line between nature and culture, and the stability attributed to nature (vs the variability attributed to culture) are themselves both *culturally drawn lines*. That is, the idea that the body is the "real," that exists "prior" to cultural inscription, so that gender simply comes to expression through inevitable effects of bodily, material determinants, is itself a cultural idea. The very idea of "nature" as a realm beyond cultural determination or human choice has a history associated with the rise of science's dominance as *the* realm that investigates why things are they way they are. The anthropologist Eduardo Vivieros de Castro shows that Amerindians have quite different beliefs about the relation between nature and culture: rather than seeing nature as an invariant universal that then has different cultures inscribed on top of it, Amerindians see "'culture' . . . as the form of the universal, and 'nature' . . . as the particular."[2] But not only humans have culture; animals (especially predators) do too. Rather than imagining, as many Westerners do, that there's a single world seen by different people and beings in many different ways, Amerindians claim that "all beings see ('represent') the world *in the same way*; what changes is *the world they see*." Where humans see blood, jaguars see beer.[3] The distinction between nature, as the realm of shared, universal, objective properties, and culture, as the realm of particular, historical, contingent properties, thus shifts radically.

This distinction between nature and culture is one of the binary distinctions that, theorists argue, undergird, well, *culture*. Other binary distinctions include male/female, heterosexual/homosexual, good/evil, reason/emotion, white/black, and so on. These binary distinctions seek to organize reality and categorize it according to whether it is *this* or *that*. Those ways of organizing reality are also ways of valuing reality. Heterosexuality is natural, while homosexuality is a perversion of nature, some think. Heterosexuality and homosexuality are both natural, while repressing sexuality is a perversion of nature, others might argue. In both these

2. Vivieros de Castro, *Cannibal Metaphysics*, 56.

3. Ibid., 71.

examples, nature is a valued term expressing a sense that something *ought* to be a certain way.

Contrast the famous line from Thomas Hobbes that life in a state of nature is "nasty, brutish, and short." Here, the assumption is that culture has to subdue and organize nature to avoid the latter's brutality. Subduing natural passions is the foundation of civilization, he assumes. "The noble savage," on the other hand, is a racial trope that manages to combine a high valuation of nature with a sense of the tragic but inevitable encroachment of "civilization" and "progress." As these examples suggest, it's not the case that nature is always valued over culture, or vice versa, whenever that distinction organizes reality. But, at the same time, that distinction is one of the fundamental organizing categories that structures our interpretation of reality and our sense of what is right and good and the way things ought to be, and what isn't.

These categories organize reality for us long before we become conscious of their power. By the time we become full participants in social life, we have been fully enculturated. The distinction between male and female, or the distinction between heterosexual and homosexual, has come to seem no more than the natural way of distinguishing different categories or types of human beings. Forgotten, because we never knew, is how those categories came to seem so natural and inevitable—the process of training that taught us which bathroom to use, how to express our gender, or what the significance of sexuality is to a human being's self-understanding. These ways of being in the world are fundamental to everyday, lived existence. They affect how one styles one's hair, how one throws a ball, which body parts one covers, which body parts one removes hair from, what kind of underwear one wears, which stores one shops in, how close one is comfortable being to the bodies of strangers, whether one sits or stands to use the bathroom, the inflection of one's voice, and so many other things. And that's without even considering how one's personality is shaped by reactions to one's perceived or presumed gender identity!

As theorists of sex and gender argue, it is also a historically contingent fact that the idea of a sexual orientation organized around gender distinctions became so important. In the last chapter, I mentioned in passing that arguments from historical distance point out that the idea of a homosexual orientation would have been foreign to the cultural milieus within which the Bible was written. Homosexuality, as designating an exclusive, lifelong orientation only toward persons of the same sex, making up the *identity* of the person to whom the orientation attaches, is given its current form through the classification practices of medical and psychiatric scientists. The notion that homosexuality expresses an identity, who a person *really* is, that requires authentic expression, is also culturally contingent (as is the importance given to authenticity as a value).[4]

Sensibilities of this kind express what theorists of sex and gender refer to as a process of naturalization, the way our organizing categories seem transparent to (what we call) nature, expressive simply of the way things are, not culturally determined. It is *natural* that humans are divided into men and women, and that social and sexual life reflects that division, we assume. But these binary divisions don't, and can't, fully encapsulate all of reality. They are unstable when pushed. Indeed, they are fundamentally unstable: they have to be produced, and reinforced, over

---

4. That doesn't mean that there haven't been people historically who we would think of as being in same-gender or same-sex relationships. But the *meaning* of that status, and its significance for how we think personhood, shifts.

and over again. "You make me feel like a natural woman," sings Aretha Franklin—reminding us that being a "natural woman" is the outcome, the result (not the starting point) of cultural productions of gender and heterosexuality. Theorists of sex and gender also emphasize how few people—if any—live lives fully captured by ideals of gender distinction. One need only look around one's own neighborhood or social milieu to find that there are many different ways of being gendered. Many, maybe even most, people live lives that aren't fully consistent with the ideology of gender.

Pointing out such instability—that binary divisions don't successfully and consistently capture all of reality—is part of a process of *denaturalization*. Denaturalization renders visible the culturally constructed nature of our basic organizing categories, thus limiting their power and efficacy. Denaturalization is part of the process of destabilizing, in order to change, binary and hierarchical distinctions between men and women, straight and gay, cisgender and transgender. For many theorists of sex and gender, denaturalization is a fundamental form of *queering*. Showing that binary categories are unstable and incomplete loosens their hold on us, it is hoped.

Denaturalization is typically combined with another, closely connected strategy: anti-essentialism. Worries about essentialism with regard to gender and sexuality became particularly important in some feminist debates in the 1970s and 1980s. Wildly oversimplifying, the distinction arises because of the possible incompatibility of two popular feminist strategies: liberal, or equality feminism, and difference feminism. Liberal, or equality feminism, argues that women need the same opportunities as men have. They need to be able to participate in the workforce on equal terms; they need to be assigned the same rights as men by the state; and they need to get equal pay and equal opportunities for power, promotion, and monetary accumulation. Difference feminism seeks rather to value more highly traits and practices stereotypically associated with women: nurturing behavior, emotional wisdom, and reproduction. Because difference feminism values the traits stereotypically associated with women, it seems to liberal feminists to concede too much ground. Isn't difference feminism effectively admitting that patriarchy is correct about what women are like? Doesn't difference feminism, in effect, assume that women are *essentially* more nurturing, more emotional, more oriented toward relationships than achievement? Yet difference feminists point out that the opportunities valued by liberal feminism are themselves part of larger cultural, social, economic, and political systems of inequality and injustice. It's all well and good to have women as CEO's of Fortune 500 companies, but isn't the equivalence between money, achievement, and value what really needs to change?

Alongside these debates ran two others. The needs, wants, and experiences of women vary widely, not only between cultures, but within specific societies. Who are the women that feminism is for? Do black women and white women in the USA share a common core of "women's" experience, or should white women's participation in the oppression of black women and black men be weighed more heavily? What about the relationship between white, Latinx, and black women in the USA, and typically Arab or Southeast Asian women in the countries colonized and bombed by the USA? The partial detente that followed these debates can be simply encapsulated: all women, trans* and cis, are different from each other; they do not share an essential nature or set of characteristics. Just like cis women, trans* women do not share a common experience, nature, or set of characteristics; determining what or who counts as a "real" woman (as trans-exclusionary radical feminists, sexists, and misogynists of all genders do), targets both cis and trans* women, and is itself an inherently anti-feminist act.

Gender is not then an expression of a stable, unified, inward self but, in Judith Butler's famous words, "a stylized repetition of acts."[5] Gender is not the expression of one's core being, anatomically determined and culturally expressed. Rather, gender expresses the way we learn to behave, the way we are read and interpreted by others, the way signs of gender mark our bodies, our movements, our behaviors, our clothes. We understand gender because we have seen others *do* gender, and we ourselves learn to *do* gender in the same way. Heteronormativity, the naturalization of the sociopolitical system of heterosexuality within patriarchy, teaches us that there are two and only two sexes whose anatomy or genes determine their gender, and who are naturally oriented to each other in terms of romantic and sexual desire in a way that finds its highest fulfillment and aim in marriage and reproduction. But heteronormativity is not natural in the way it pretends to be; it is the effect of a cultural system that enforces heterosexuality throughout. Indeed, Butler argued that heterosexuality is the effect of the prohibition against homosexuality, so that in a sense, homosexuality comes first, as that which is forbidden in order to give meaning, stability, and coherence to heterosexuality.

Butler's argument sounds counterintuitive to many, but it reflects the particularity of our current Western organization of sex, sexuality, and desire. Heterosexuality and homosexuality are both modern words, not just modern concepts—in fact, the word homosexuality was invented before heterosexuality, and heterosexuality originally

5. Butler, *Gender Trouble*, 191.

designated someone whose sexuality was heterogeneous relative to the norm—that is, someone who we now would say was *not* heterosexual. Gender inversion—the masculine woman, the effeminate man—was the more common way of understanding same-sex oriented sexual behavior in the preceding years, whereas we now quite firmly separate gender identity from sexual orientation. As is widely recognized, ancient Greece, and Rome during the early centuries of the common era, had little difficulty with the idea of men having some form of sexual relationship with adolescent boys; the relevant distinction was not the gender of the sexual object but the social status of the "active" or insertive partner relative to that of the "passive" partner. An anti-essentialist lens clarifies that these same-sex relations are *not* what we think of as homosexuality, while a denaturalizing approach reminds us that neither our categories (gay, heterosexual, nonbinary, woman, etc.) nor ancient Greek or Roman categories (*molles*, *tribades*, *malthakoi*, and so on) are *natural*. They are all produced by various cultural forces (which also affect the way genes and tendencies come to expression) in ways that mark us from within, in ways we can neither fully recognize nor control.

The nature or nurture question is, then, the wrong question, because it falsely assumes that the two can be separated from each other, and it fails to recognize the particularity of our own organizing categories for gender and sexuality. But contemporary distinctions between homosexuality and heterosexuality, as well as the focus on sex, gender, and sexuality in general, also brings with it much deeper assumptions about the constitutive place of sexuality, romantic love, and marriage in human existence, as well as the centrality of gender identity and sexual orientation to personhood as such. This leads to deep disagreements between those who accept those basic assumptions, and seek only to extend greater social recognition to otherwise "normal" queer, trans*, and nonbinary people, and those who believe that the entire system of recognition, validation, and determination of what is "normal," is the problem. And so, we must turn our attention to the question of queer.

## THE QUESTION OF QUEER

Anti-essentialist analyses that seek denaturalization sit somewhat uneasily with typical strategies of arguing for acceptance and inclusion of queer, trans*, and nonbinary people in relation to the state as well as within many churches. Arguments for acceptance and inclusion are often predicated on a sometimes unstated, sometimes explicit assumption that queer, trans*, and nonbinary people are *born that way*. They can't help it (by implication: they would if they could), and their gender or sexual identity expresses their most authentic self. They seek only to express and fulfill their deepest longings in the same way that heterosexual, married people already do. In the United States, Justice Kennedy's widely praised opinion legalizing same-sex marriage brings together many of these assumptions. "The nature of marriage is that, through its enduring bond, two persons together can find other freedoms, such as expression, intimacy, and spirituality." Marriage is the context of care for children, and the children of same-sex unions need to be protected from the experience of children of unmarried couples, who "suffer the stigma of knowing their families are somehow lesser . . . relegated through no fault of their own to a more difficult and uncertain family life." Marriage has "transcendent purposes." Indeed, "no union is more profound than marriage, for it embodies the highest ideals of love, fidelity, devotion, sacrifice, and family." The petitioners, he writes, "respect [marriage] so deeply that they seek to find its fulfillment for themselves. Their hope is not to be condemned to live in loneliness, excluded from one of civilization's oldest institutions. They ask for equal dignity in the eyes of the law."[6] Who could resist such a pathetic (albeit bathetic to some) plea on behalf of same-sex partners and their children? Condemned otherwise to live in loneliness, their children stigmatized, their capacities for devotion, sacrifice, and spirituality unrecognized and unfulfilled, the state *recognizes* the pleas of its citizens for equal rights and dignity and so grants those rights. Justice Kennedy sees marriage as "embodying the highest ideals"— whose ideals, and the highest in which sense, one might ask? Are married people not lonely? Are all unmarried people lonely? What is spirituality, anyway?

These questions may seem like quibbles, but they are not. Kennedy's arguments embody the liberal versions of the assumptions that structure many debates over sexuality. Some values are higher than others; those values deserve social and legal sanction; those values are oriented toward reproduction and the fulfillment of two individuals within a legally established framework; marriage is about two (and only two) persons coming together in a "high," "transcendent," and "spiritual" way. The fulfillment of one's inmost self takes place in marriage; those who seek to marry someone of the "same" sex seek only to be allowed into the already-existing institution of marriage rather than to change it in any way.

Kennedy's language is the language of normativity, the circuit of mutually reinforcing assumptions around what's normal, what's legitimate, what the state should promote, whose interests the state should protect, and so on. Kennedy tries to avoid violating the separation of church and

6. All from Justice Anthony M. Kennedy's opinion for the Supreme Court in *Obergefell v. Hodges.*

state by talking about transcendence and spirituality in very general terms, emptied, he hopes, of any particular religious referent while still invoking a sense of something important and valuable, irreducible to say, *sexual* desire (indeed, the decision talks about individual autonomy and intimacy rather than directly about sex). "From their beginning to their most recent page, the annals of human history reveal the transcendent importance of marriage. The lifelong union of a man and a woman always has promised nobility and dignity to all persons, without regard to their station in life. Marriage is sacred to those who live by their religions and offers unique fulfillment to those who find meaning in the secular realm. Its dynamic allows two people to find a life that could not be found alone, for a marriage becomes greater than just the two persons. Rising from the most basic human needs, marriage is essential to our most profound hopes and inspirations."[7] Having claimed that marriage has "promised nobility and dignity to all persons," Kennedy only a few pages later concedes that women were long legally subjugated to men in marriage.

In recounting the history of criminalization of same-sex sexuality, Kennedy interprets criminalization as disallowing "homosexuals . . . dignity in their own distinct identity. A truthful declaration by same-sex couples of what was in their hearts had to remain unspoken."[8] Dignity in identity, telling the truth about what's in one's heart. These ideals of selfhood are themselves deeply contentious, even when veiled in liberal cant. Is who one chooses to have sex with an expression of one's "dignity" in one's "identity," or are the ideals of dignity and identity the means by which social privileges are extended to the supposedly deserving and denied to the purportedly undeserving?

7. Ibid.
8. Ibid.

The vision of selfhood embedded in Justice Kennedy's reasoning is the classic liberal subject who freely determines "himself" in the context of a social order that respects and honors his choices because they proceed from his true and real self. The classic liberal subject possesses himself and uses his labor to transform nature into property; he is thus fundamentally distinguished from slaves, who have both their person and their labor stolen from them, and from indigenous people, who typically don't see nature as property. He is the subject of the rights of man (or Man) in the thought of the Enlightenment. He is normatively white, male, propertied and rational. The liberal subject has the characteristics that he has because he is contrasted with other human beings who don't share those characteristics, who fail to be as authentically and fully human as he is.

This normative subject is the one against whom, implicitly, nonnormative subjects of all kinds are measured and fall short (some more than others), even though in reality, it's not the case that some human beings are self-possessing, self-determining, autonomous subjects and others are not. In reality, all human beings experience loss, lack, and fragmentation. We all live and form ourselves within contexts we did not ourselves choose, in dependence on others. Yet the imaginary vision of the truly free subject continues to haunt us as a specter of possibility against which different people fall short in different ways. White propertied men too fall short when they fail to conform to the standards of normative masculinity in terms of their gender performance, for instance—but even the most "normative" human being can be made such only by a process of abstraction, a snapshot taken at a specific moment that erases both particularity and the time across which human life takes place. Put differently: the normative subject is a fiction, but it's a destructive fiction that plays a role in the

63

unjust distribution of social goods *even though no one* really *is* such a subject.

One of the most famous definitions of "queer" calls it "an identity without an essence" that is "defined wholly relationally, by its distance to and difference from the normative."[9] Rather than following the line of Justice Kennedy's argument, that the normativity of marriage needs to be extended to include same-sex couples, this definition instead values queer as "*whatever* is at odds with the normal, the legitimate, the dominant. *There is nothing in particular to which it necessarily refers.*"[10] David Halperin, who offers the definition, sees "queer" as potentially encompassing a wide range of nonnormative sexualities, but his intent here is not to define queer just right, in order to designate just the right people, nor to recognize different sexual identities as such (though those differences are real). The key, Halperin argues, is not accurate naming (queer vs. gay or lesbian vs. homosexual, for instance) but "careful evaluation of the *strategic* functioning" of language, paying attention to "the specific *effects* our terminology of choice will produce when it is deployed—to understand what, concretely, it will make happen."[11] Our language participates in sociopolitical processes that determine who gets the full protection of the state (straight white men who don't suffer from mental illness), who bears the brunt of the state's violence (black people, undocumented migrants, people with mental illness, and Arabs and Afghanis). If queer people invest in the language that Kennedy uses, queer people are also investing in the kind of citizen, the kind of person, that Kennedy's opinion designates as the sort of person who deserves state protection.

9. Halperin, *Saint Foucault*, 61.

10. Ibid., 62.

11. Ibid., 63.

As may be clear at this point, I share Halperin's skepticism of the power of getting names just right—as though accurately naming every sexual choice and gender identity will revolutionize a sociopolitical order that has gender identity and various forms of hierarchical differentiation at its heart, as Julia Serano points out regarding transmisogyny.[12] Halperin goes on to list many of the disadvantages of using the term queer: it's unspecific (which is also an advantage, he thinks); it pretends to inclusiveness and so can't acknowledge differences in practices, forms of identification, race, gender, nationality, and so on; it's sexually unspecific (that is, it takes the "sex" out of "homosexual"); and it potentially participates in generational and terminological wars in which right naming becomes a substitute for transformational political practice.[13] The disadvantages Halperin names are quite similar to those identified by people who dislike the term queer for the apparent claim to universalism it contains, a universalism which seems to privilege those who would call themselves queer (often white and Western) over those who might not themselves so understand their lives, identities, or sexual practices. Feminist and lesbian thinkers have worried that "queer" becomes a way to make women's sexuality, and especially lesbian sexuality, not merely invisible but unfashionable, retrograde, unsexy compared to the coolness, flexibility, fluidity, and non-gender-specificity of queer. At the time of writing, "queer" may itself be undergoing a similar recategorization as unfashionable and outdated, to be replaced by trans* studies.

In 1997, Cathy J. Cohen published an article that remains, I think, unsurpassed in its capacity to analyze the conditions under which "queer politics" is, or is not, a

12. Serano, *Whipping Girl*.

13. Ibid., 64–65.

useful way of looking at these questions (and that has one of the most gorgeously memorable titles of any academic article I've read): "Punks, Bulldaggers, and Welfare Queens: The Radical Potential of Queer Politics?" Cohen argues that a queer politics focused on the difference between "heterosexual and everything 'queer'" won't make up a radical queer politics—won't be enough to unsettle dominant distributions of power.

Instead, we need "a politics where the *nonnormative* and *marginal* position of punks, bulldaggers, and welfare queens, for example, is the basis for progressive transformative coalition work."[14] Queer politics, if it is to be of any use (Cohen specifies that she does not identify herself as a queer political activist) needs to be about something more and broader than a single-issue politics focused on the difference between those who are heterosexual and cisgender and everyone else, as though everyone who lives a "heterosexual" life also lives a hetero*normative* life. Instead, Cohen emphasizes that heteronormativity isn't available to all heterosexuals: some presumptive heterosexuals (like Black single mothers) are stigmatized as aberrant and nonnormative. Hortense Spillers famously argues that the entire normative sex-gender system in the United States has never been available to black people, who, when brought as slaves, were robbed both of existing kinship ties and of the *right* to kinship. The normative form of heterosexuality, in which a child belongs to a mother and a father, was a possibility violently foreclosed for the enslaved.[15]

"Queer," as Cohen points out, also carries with it an assumption of fluidity and freedom from all identity categories that doesn't always apply or appeal to LGBT people of color, who often have reasons for attachment to "stable

14. Cohen, "Punks, Bulldaggers, and Welfare Queens," 438.
15. Spillers, "Mama's Baby, Papa's Maybe."

categories and named communities whose histories have been structured by shared resistance to oppression."[16] Political action for significant change needs to be organized around multiple vectors of oppression, dis/advantage, and stigmatization; otherwise, the stigmatization and imposed deviance of some heterosexuals, particularly those who are poor, undocumented, or black, will be invisible.

Despite their real differences, Cohen and Halperin share a sense that if queer is to be a valuable category, it will be so if and only if it is about the many ways in which people living vastly different forms of life are stigmatized, rendered deviant and dangerous. "Queer," if useful, stands for those against whom dominant social understandings of the normative develop. The exact focus of such operations of power will vary at different times. When Cohen and Halperin were writing, welfare and HIV/AIDS played significant roles in public discourse; now stigmatization of Muslim    extremists/refugees/migrants/terrorists/Islamists (all slid into associative relationship with each other) has become much more important to European and US politics. At the same time, #BlackLivesMatter—an organization founded by queer Black women—agitates for the end of anti-Black police violence as well as for changes in prison practices, restorative justice, and related issues.

Halperin and Cohen clearly diverge on the issue of the *sexuality* of queer, though. For Halperin, it's important that queer retain a link to specifically sexual stigma, even though that stigma can attach to many who are "heterosexual" (as in the case of some sex workers); for Cohen, it's not the form of stigma but the type of political action undertaken that determines the possibilities and limits of coalitions seeking transformation. The queer politics she wants will link different forms of marginalization—"ideological,

16. Cohen, "Punks, Bulldaggers, and Welfare Queens," 450.

social, political, and economic"—to each other for the sake of a broadly transformational politics.[17] Whether or not the stigmatization has a specifically sexual element is not so important to her.

The patient reader may now be thinking, "That's all well and good, but isn't this chapter supposed to be about queer *theology*?" We saw above that anti-essentialism and denaturalization are strategies for making the contingency of our current organizations of sex, gender, and sexuality visible. We also encountered two different ways of thinking about the relationship between the state, politics, and sexuality. In one, embedded in Justice Kennedy's discourse, the state's distribution of rights and recognition touches on the highest aspirations of humanity as such, through the institution of marriage. Marriage is a question of autonomy, dignity, nobility, and truth-telling; it's about the relation between one's inmost self and the social. In the other, queer is about (and against) just the kinds of assumptions that structure Justice Kennedy's text. Queer sets itself against state distribution of rights and recognition; instead, it seeks transformation of the very social, political, and economic structures *within which state distribution of rights and recognition appears to be the goal of political action. Queer*, according to Halperin, is not abut identity but about a relation to power. While less fond of the term queer, Cohen agrees: queer must be for and about those who are nonnormative and marginal.

We should now begin to see whether, and if so, how queer is compatible with some Christian ways of talking about human beings. Christian theologians and ethicists are often quite invested in producing normative visions of human beings: this is what makes us human, this is how human beings *ought* to be. Human beings have an inalienable

17. Cohen, "Punks, Bulldaggers, and Welfare Queens," 482.

dignity that should be respected and fostered, because they are made in the image of God. Much like Justice Kennedy's arguments for state recognition, theologians and ethicists have argued for church recognition of same-sex marriage on grounds of dignity, love, and holiness. Is *that* really what queer Christian theology should be about? I want to suggest that, following Halperin and Cohen, the answer to that question is no. Yes, churches can and should sanction same-sex marriages if they remain in the marriage business at all, but queer theology is not needed to make that argument.

The sanctioning of same-sex marriage takes place within already existing institutions that distribute rights and recognition in line with their normative visions of humanity (this is how human beings *ought* to be). But investing in normative visions of humanity inevitably means distinguishing between the dignified, rights-having, loving individual, and the undignified, rights-violating, unloving individual who threatens the social, political, or theological order within which the former individual gains recognition. The undignified, rights-violating, unloving individual needs to be shut out, even imprisoned, in order to protect the dignified, rights-having, loving individual. The lofty language of dignity and rights often has the effect, in practice, of *denying* dignity and rights to those who don't fit the vision of the human that such language assumes. Undocumented migrants, terrorists, people who sell drugs, and sex workers are *themselves* denying their dignity, in this way of thinking. They are threats to *our* rights; they are not people to whom rights belong. As Halperin suggested regarding queer, so with language of rights and dignity: we need to look at the effects of language, at what it makes happen. This doesn't mean that arguments for rights and recognition should never be made, but that such arguments are at best a risky, temporary compromise within a wider practice of transformation, not themselves the aim of queer politics and queer theology.

Nor should the aim of queer politics or queer theology simply be anti-essentialism or denaturalization. Anti-essentialism and denaturalization are better understood as *starting points* for further work and reflection. As queer theorist Eve Kosofsky Sedgwick pointed out in 1996, it's not particularly "shocking that ideologies contradict themselves, that simulacra don't have originals, [and] gender representations are artificial."[18] Noting that contemporary formations of sexuality aren't natural is important, but it does little if anything to loosen the hold those formations have on us. Even Halperin, who strenuously argues for the difference between, say, ancient Greek views of same-sex relations and contemporary ones, admits that his knowledge of the contingency of current formations of sexuality has little effect on his experience of himself.[19] The conditions under which anti-essentialism and denaturalization would be effective as *strategies* rather than *starting points* are precisely the conditions that anti-essentialism and denaturalization do most to contest.

Let me explain that somewhat surprising point. Anti-essentialism and denaturalization are both strategies that draw attention to contingency. Things don't *have to* be the way they are; they could be otherwise. The way they are isn't determined by an immutable nature (denaturalization) nor by the real being of things (anti-essentialism). Instead, the way things are is the result of contingent processes, even though we often experience the way things are as natural and (to some extent) unchanging. That's a helpful and important point.

18. Sedgwick, "Paranoid Reading," 141. See also Tonstad, "Limits of Inclusion."

19. Halperin, *One Hundred Years*, 53.

But denaturalization and anti-essentialism would only effectively *change* the way things are (rather than point out that things could be other than they are) if we were self-transparent, rational, autonomous individuals who, recognizing that something could be otherwise, were capable of predicting the outcomes of our actions in such a way that the result would be straightforwardly *making* things otherwise. For denaturalization and anti-essentialism to achieve change, our recognition that things could be otherwise would need to alter or destroy our investment in the way things are, the way our selves are formed at the deepest levels within heteronormativity, patriarchy, racism, and so on. The moment we put it like that, though, we recognize that heteronormativity, patriarchy, and racism live *within us*, are part of us (even if we are targeted by them)—and knowing that they live within us doesn't end their hold on us—because we *aren't* self-transparent, rational, autonomous individuals. Recognizing that heteronormativity, patriarchy, and racism shape both ourselves and the world we live in is certainly important. The diagnostic tools of critical thought help us to see that they so shape us and how they do so—both in the sense of what about us they shape, and in the sense of what strategies they depend on. Awareness of the world's deformation by what many theologians call the powers and principalities—powerful, destructive forces that nonetheless shape us at deep levels, and from which we long to be freed—is akin to a process of conversion or a mystical experience. Subsequently, one sees the world and one's own experience through new eyes. Or, perhaps one has always known about these deforming powers because one has always been targeted by them. Even so, acting to break their hold on the world by reshaping it and oneself, one's being in the world, and the social, economic, and political systems that these powers foster, remains a lifelong project that starts anew each day. It's never complete or finished.

What's more, the presumed efficiency of anti-essentialism and denaturalization derives from the sense that ideology demands consistency—that is, that demonstrating contradiction, incoherence, and incompletion in a thought system will effectively disempower the thought system. But as many thinkers (including Butler, Spillers, Halperin, and Sedgwick) have shown, contradiction, incoherence, and inconsistency are the *means by which* contemporary ideological/sexual/social formations stay in place. Thus, pointing out inconsistency and incoherence won't necessarily make these powers and principalities ineffective, even though showing their inconsistency and incoherence is important.[20] As Halperin says, "fighting entrenched social agencies and practices with nothing but ideology is not a game you can win (as feminists have discovered), because culturally dominant forces can always reconfigure whatever interpretation of yourself you may put forward to suit their own interests."[21] Minoritized subjects should absolutely put forward their own self-representations, but no guarantee of such representational efficacy can be provided. Showing *how* a homophobic discourse works can be part of making its strategies apparent; it can help to identify quilting points for resistance and change; it can even help to make its strategies less effective, although it does not dissolve their power. Demonstrating inconsistency and incoherence is part of working for change, but such demonstration is not the end point of a process of social, or theological, transformation.

If queer theology isn't about coming up with normative visions of humanity or concluding that gender and

20. For more on this, see Tonstad, "Ambivalent Loves," especially 6–7.

21. Halperin, *One Hundred Years*, 52.

sexual identities are constructed, what is it about? At this point we need to introduce the theologian without whom the term "queer theology" would have little content or meaning: Marcella Althaus-Reid (1952–2009). Althaus-Reid produced two major books, *Indecent Theology* and *The Queer God*, as well as numerous articles, book chapters, and edited volumes. While Althaus-Reid was born and raised in Argentina, she spent many years in Scotland, where she became the first woman professor of theology at New College, University of Edinburgh. Althaus-Reid was trained in liberation theology and feminist theology, but she combined and went beyond both. Liberation theology, for Althaus-Reid, did not go far enough. While it recognized the intimate relationship between structures of oppression and impoverishment and Christianity (especially European colonial Christianity as brought to Latin America and US-American forms of colonization on grounds of "manifest destiny"), liberation theology wasn't always clear about the poor it sought to be *for*—who the poor are, and what their needs are. Althaus-Reid, in memorable and poetic prose, pointed out that the poor are sexual beings too, whose lives are constrained not only by ideologies of capitalism but also by sexual ideologies and sexual theologies. Feminist theology too had not done enough, Althaus-Reid argued, to move beyond the fixity of gender and sexuality. Searching for feminine images of God is all well and good, but often such images become no more than adjuncts to a divine masculinity that becomes increasingly fixed the more it is denied. Feminist theologians in Latin America had, according to Althaus-Reid, been shunted off to the side, allowed to say something about Mary or women's experience, but never permitted fundamentally to challenge (or even really to address) central theological categories like God, Christ, or salvation.

73

But wait. I have lectured on Althaus-Reid in various theology classes, and I usually have to start by saying what I should say now as well: strictly speaking, Althaus-Reid's work can't be talked about in a classroom set up like an ordinary theology classroom at a fancy university, or in the dry academic prose I just offered. Althaus-Reid should be talked about in a leather bar, by those who (as she said) go to salsa bars with rosaries in their pockets, or even more accurately: Althaus-Reid's theology shouldn't be talked *about,* reduced to an object of analysis. Let's try this again.

"To be a theologian is to respond to urges of parental divine ingratitude, and in a way, nothing could be more true."[22] "Is theology the art of putting your hands under the skirts of God?"[23] Theology is the art of "going to bed with God while avoiding full sex."[24] "Theology is the art of a critical bisexual action and reflection on God and humanity."[25] Theology is *art,* representation. It's a way of organizing reality, both to reflect and change it. Theological writing (and reading), like all human practices, are *bodied practices.* They are undertaken by bodied beings who, on the level of the text, are often barely able to talk about "the body." Theologians produce products (theological texts) with their bodies, yet the page of a theological text often pretends to be as far from the body as anything can be: discourses of abstraction laboriously handwritten or typed, perhaps with aching wrists and shoulders, seated somewhere or other (perhaps in one's favorite cheap Ikea office chair, marked by the claws of naughty cats, writing on an Apple computer, and so in direct relation to other animals and global capitalism,

22. Althaus-Reid, *Queer God,* 44.

23. Althaus-Reid, "Queer I Stand: Lifting the Skirts of God," in Althaus-Reid and Isherwood, eds., *Sexual Theologian,* 99.

24. Althaus-Reid, *Indecent Theology,* 23.

25. Althaus-Reid, *Queer God,* 1.

including exploitation of humans and natural resources). Is the writer waiting for a lover to arrive? Is there perhaps a child wailing to be fed? A domestic worker in the background, freeing the writer for a few hours? Has one gone to a library or coffee shop or bar or park to escape, or to be in the company of strangers, as an antidote to loneliness? How is the food that one eats or the coffee that one drinks to sustain the writing of theology paid for? What would happen if one wrote theology and allowed the writing to reflect its own conditions, its own truths? What if, in Althaus-Reid's memorable image, one sat down to write theology without wearing underwear? What if theology were about reality?

The task of theology is to "deconstruct a moral order which is based on a heterosexual construction of reality, which organizes not only categories of approved social and divine interactions but of economic ones too."[26] Theology, in short, is about sex, money, and God. Theology is about bodies meeting bodies, and where bodies meet are also images, representations, imaginations, fantasies. Bodies are sustained by money, or what money can buy; bodies are threatened by the lack of money, or what money can pay for. For Althaus-Reid, all theology is sexual theology, all theology is economic theology, and all theology is implicated in the socioeconomic and sexual systems within which it emerges. During the brutal military dictatorship in Argentina, the Plaza del Mayo outside the cathedral in Buenos Aires resounded with the shout: "They were taken away alive, we want them back alive." And inside the cathedral, the church continued its business, feeding the body of Christ to people and promising resurrection under the benevolent gaze of the virgin Mary.

Althaus-Reid clearly recognizes the dual status of the normative subject as both fictional and destructive:

26. Althaus-Reid, *Indecent Theology*, 2.

"Heterosexual women need to come out of their closet like anybody else, speaking the truth about their lives, heavily domesticated by patriarchal definitions of what it is to be a heterosexual, monogamous, faithful woman with a motherly vocation."[27] As Cohen and Halperin recognize, the issue for queer thinking isn't heterosexuality vs. all other sexualities. The issue is heterosexuality as *ideology*, as theology, as normative sociopolitical and, crucially, economic system.

Heterosexuality as a system doesn't deal with truth. Theological heterosexuality deals with fictions, ideas of what human beings ought to be like that are divorced and distanced from the reality of human, bodied, sexual life. Yet those fictions get used against people. Poor women are called indecent or undeserving if their lives don't conform to heterosexual, middle class ideologies of sexual behavior. They are often called undeserving by politicians whose own lives bear no trace of the decency they seek to impose on others.

Meanwhile, those who seek to be for and on the side of the poor often don't recognize the complexity of people's lives. They want to be for the poor of their imagination, the abstract poor, not the poor of reality. But "in reality, heterosexuality makes of every courageous human being a Queer, indecent person. Only very hypocritical people may claim to live according to the rules, *contra natura*, of heterosexual politics and theology. Deep in our hearts, we are all 'Queer Nation' needing to come out and denounce that human beings live and love according to reality, and not Christian indexes on morals."[28] Althaus-Reid calls on theologians to tell the truth as well. What would have happened if the great 20th century theologian Karl Barth had

27. Ibid., 46.
28. Ibid., 120.

told the truth about how boring and unsatisfying he found marriage, as he sat in his office or vacationed with Charlotte von Kirschbaum (not his wife) while writing his 14-volume *Church Dogmatics*,[29] in which he discussed the way man is "A" and woman is "B" so that he "precedes and is superior in relation to woman" who "is woman, and therefore B, and therefore behind and subordinate to man"?[30] Theology talks about a God the Father and a God the Son, but pretends fatherhood and sonship have nothing to do with sex or gender even as Christianity has also (but not only) been a system of patriarchy throughout its history. What would theology say if it told *these* truths? *That* is the question of queer theology.

29. Ibid., 49, 120.
30. Barth, *Church Dogmatics* III/4, 170–71.

# 4

# MONEY, SEX, AND GOD

*Althaus-Reid's Queer Theology*

IF THEOLOGY TOLD THE truth, it would speak of bodies, of flesh. Althaus-Reid's theology is thoroughly materialist, both in assumptions and content. She worries about the false abstractions whereby theological categories become solidified, almost as if they were real. Solidified or thingified theological categories can then become touchstones for judging and organizing people. The "reality" of the solidified theological category or concept becomes the standard by which other, actually real realities (people and their messy lives) are judged unreal, or insufficient, or imperfect. This is the "reason why dogmas exist in the first place, to reorder reality,"[1] she says. Through the social and economic processes that dogmas reflect and keep in place, human beings misrecognize their relations to each other.

1. Althaus-Reid, *Indecent Theology*, 45.

Such an argument has deep historical roots. In the mid-19th century, the German philosopher Ludwig Feuerbach argued that religion, specifically Christianity, reflects just such a process of misrecognition in relation to God. In Christianity, human beings misrecognize themselves. They take their own features, capacities, and activities, abstract them from their actual existence in human beings, and attribute them to God. So human beings are loving, knowing creatures with a capacity for recognizing justice and acting ethically. Rather than recognizing the essential humanness of those characteristics, human beings take love, knowledge, justice, power, and goodness, abstract them (as theological omni-categories: God is omni-benevolent, all-knowing or omniscient, the universal judge, all-powerful or omnipotent, and goodness itself) and assign them to God, who stands over against humanity in a sense. Humanity is thus alienated from its own reality, and needs instead to recognize its own true nature.

Feuerbach was hugely influential in his day—his major work, *The Essence of Christianity*, was translated into English by George Eliot—but he is especially remembered today because of his significance to Karl Marx. For Marx, religion is a fundamental form of the mystification that capitalism requires, where relationships between people are misrecognized as relations between things. Marx writes that "the criticism of religion is the prerequisite of all criticism."[2] Marx thinks that critique of religion is completed in Feuerbach's work. Fundamentally, Feuerbach recognized that religion is not about God, but about human beings and our relationships with one another. But for Marx, Feuerbach has not gone far enough. He hasn't recognized the social,

2. Marx, "Contribution to a Critique of Hegel's Philosophy of Right," in *Early Political Writings*, 57.

inter-human basis of the split human beings produce between themselves and God.

Feuerbach, Marx thinks, rightly identified a split between an ordinary world of human existence and activity, and an imagined world in which abstractions are misrecognized as real. They agree in naming the latter as the world with which theology traffics. But Feuerbach didn't realize how splits, rifts, and contradictions *within the ordinary world of human existence and activity* form the basis for the split between the ordinary world and the imagined world. So, Marx says, it's not enough to recognize that the underlying, real truth of the Holy Family is what we now call the nuclear family (Marx calls it the bourgeois family). It's not enough to see that the real purpose of making a family holy (Mary, Joseph, and Jesus) is to sanctify a particular family form: mother, father, child. *After* that recognition, one needs to make the nuclear family itself the object of critique.[3] This is because, as Marx says in one of his most famous lines, "Philosophers have merely interpreted the world in various ways. The point is to change it."[4]

When one focuses critique on the nuclear family, it becomes clear that, socioeconomically, its meaning is twofold: social reproduction and the protection of private property under conditions of paternity uncertainty. Monogamous, reproductive, heterosexual marriage is not only, or primarily, about the highest fulfillment and love of two individuals in relation to each other, as it pretends to be, and as Justice Kennedy's words in the last chapter suggest, nor is it about self-sacrificial, unselfish love of children. When one analyzes the social and economic *functions* of monogamous, reproductive, heterosexual marriage, rather

3. Marx, "On Feuerbach," in *Early Political Writings*, 117. See also Engels, *The Origin of the Family, Private Property, and the State.*

4. Marx, "On Feuerbach," in *Early Political Writings*, 118.

than the ideology and social vision that supports such marriage, one recognizes that marriage serves two main purposes. Children are needed for the continuance and growth of capitalism: children must be born, clothed, fed, and educated, so that they, in turn, become productive workers and consumers. In most countries, the reproduction costs of these workers- and entrepreneurs-to-be are paid privately and individually, by their parents, rather than by society as a whole, even though the future of society as a whole depends on their future development into entrepreneurs, inventors, home care workers, nurses, teachers, and so on.

At the same time, the accumulation of private property is legitimized because it is required for the sake of one's children, and so given something of the sanctity and authenticity granted to the nuclear family itself. Moreover, especially before DNA testing, there's only one way for biological fathers to make sure they're passing property on to their own biological children: the enforcement of monogamy and demand of virginity before marriage for women. In effect, the sexuality and reproductive capacities of women come to belong to men, either their fathers or their husbands. So the point of the nuclear family, its what-for in contemporary capitalism, is to ensure that private property will share the apparent non-economic status of the family, its social location as a form beyond capital.

Put differently, capitalism as we know it functions as an economic system partly by way of producing or supporting familial, social, and political forms that justify themselves in terms of their distance from capitalism. Can you put a price on a mother's love? Of course not! we respond, shocked. But the economic effect of *not* putting a price on a mother's love is that a mother works for free. Capitalism needs to produce a sphere of the private, a sphere that sees itself as free from capitalism's reach, to protect its colonization of our lives. The worker that modern capitalism needed (this may be changing in the next few years with the rise of automation) was a worker who could be away from the house for much of the day, who was oriented toward the clock, who was comfortable sitting still for hours at a time in aesthetically unattractive environments, who took care of (usually) his own personal needs on his own time. Such a worker needs someone to take care of his children, his house, and his meals. That someone could be a wife, or it could be someone assigned to lower social and economic status who had few other options for earning income. This is what womanist theologian Delores Williams calls the surrogacy of black women in the United States after Reconstruction.[5]

The nuclear family's economic function, in other words, is protected by ideological misrecognition of that economic function as a *non-economic* function. The nuclear family is presented as an arena of love, personal satisfaction, and authentic fulfillment. Religion gives these arrangements an aura of holiness, divine will, and ethical responsibility. Women are to be virgins, like Mary. Women are to be mothers, like Mary. From a functional perspective, then, religion arguably helps to orient the human imagination away from the realities of human self-making, from the fact that we humans are what we do. We don't have a pre-given nature, as some animals are often presumed to have. Ants have a complex social organization, what one might even call a culture, but they don't realize that culture in the significantly varied ways that human beings do. Religion teaches us to misrecognize the source of our particular social structures by assigning them to the transcendent will of God rather than to our own doing. Thus, the possibility of changing our social arrangements is also foreclosed.

5. Williams, *Sisters*.

For Marx, religion is the basis on which human injustices are tolerated and sanctioned in reality, while being alleviated in the imagination. In another of his most famous lines, he writes, "Religion is the sigh of the oppressed creature, the heart of a heartless world, and the soul of soulless conditions. It is the *opium* of the people."[6] The illusory happiness promised by religion needs to be abolished for the sake of real human happiness, he argues. Another way of putting this: religion makes what would otherwise be recognized as intolerable, tolerable. Religion (Christianity, specifically—that's Marx's primary target) tells slaves to obey their masters and promises them a reward in heaven. Religion does reflect a sense that there is something wrong in the world—it's for that very reason that religion promises a beyond, an otherwise, another existence for human beings in abstraction and distinction from the ordinary, bodied existence of everyday social life. And in so doing, religion draws attention away from the realities of everyday, bodied social life—realities of suffering, desire, oppression, injustice in the name of justice, and so on. Or, it says that such injustices are God's will. Religion covers over the way in which those injustices are produced, *made*, in interhuman relations organized for the benefit of some and at the expense of most.

But there's another sense in which Marx connects religion and capitalism. In his analysis of the commodity, Marx says that it "appears at first sight an extremely obvious, trivial thing. But its analysis brings out that it is a very strange thing, abounding in metaphysical subtleties and theological niceties."[7] The way capitalism misrecognizes relationships

6. Marx, "Contribution, to a Critique of Hegel's Philosophy of Right," in *Early Political Writings*, 57.

7. Marx, *Capital*, 163. The word "strange" here is sometimes translated "queer"!

between people is best illustrated, Marx thinks, by theology, which invents categories (sin, salvation) and actors (God, angels) to which it then attributes independent existence. Similarly, in capitalism, people make things: objects, computers, the value of oil, derivatives, the value of social media companies. People then attribute independent existence to relations between those things. Relations between people are then understood instead as relations between things—forces, objects, accounting structures—that lie outside and to some extent beyond the control of the relationships that actually shape them, sustain them, and make them possible. This is called *commodity fetishism*.

## THEOLOGY, SEXUALITY, ECONOMY

Almost all contemporary theology responds in some way to Feuerbach and Marx, even though most theology is (as one might expect!) not atheist. Without conceding that Feuerbach and Marx are right about Christianity as such, theologians recognize that the dynamics they describe are genuine. The queer theologian asks how to make these dynamics visible, and how to shift them, because the queer theologian believes that capitalism's injustices, the nuclear family's regulation of bodies and sexuality, and the state's violent enforcement of inequality are neither the message of Christianity nor the will of God. Liberation theology emerges in part out of a narrative strand in Christianity that concerns God's liberation of the enslaved, the messages of economic and political justice associated with the prophets, and Jesus' concern for and identification with the poor, needy, and socially despised.

Queer theology reflects the way religious or theological categories, economic exchanges, and these processes of misrecognition and mystification all relate to each other, but it also makes the relation between sexual stigmatization and economic exploitation central to its analyses. Capitalism is always gendered and raced. Capitalism understands itself not to pay attention to differences of gender, sexuality, and race in the search for profit. But in reality, and as historians of capitalism have shown, capitalism always works with and through categories of gender, race, and uneven geographic development (as well as colonialism). And capitalism is, as Althaus-Reid emphasizes, a system of inequality and injustice to be combated. But Althaus-Reid isn't trying to reverse unjust power relationships, or to move queers and queer theology from margin to center: "Terrible is the fate of theologies from the margin when they want to be accepted by the center," she says.[8] She wants to interrupt and transform the whole reality within which people's economic and sexual lives and relationships are organized and classified in theological terms, made coherent, given story lines or scripts to try to live up to, no matter how impossible the fulfillment of such story lines may be.

Althaus-Reid distinguishes, therefore, between indecent theology or queer theology, and T-Theology. By T-Theology, she means theology that wants to impose and keep in place a sexual-economic-religious system that does not have the capacity to wrestle with the complexity of people's lives—that, indeed, devalues such complexity. T-Theology is a grand imperial narrative of power. It seeks to classify all of reality systematically. In other words, it tries to provide holiness scripts for people's sexual and romantic lives, and by identifying what is decent and God-willed, it produces the indecent, that which (it pretends) is against God's will. T-Theology contributes religious stigmatization to economic and social oppression. It teaches people that there are values higher than the flourishing of people, and

8. Althaus-Reid and Isherwood, "Thinking Theology," 304.

it then enforces those values violently and genocidally—Althaus-Reid is thinking here especially of the way colonial expansion in Latin America was justified by the need to bring Christianity to the indigenous inhabitants, who were stigmatized on the basis of their religious and sexual practices.

There is an especially horrifying story about this that was much discussed by queer theorists in the 1990s. Jonathan Goldberg, for example, says: "I take as an originary moment in the history of the making of America what happened two days before Balboa first laid eyes on the Pacific Ocean. In a Panamanian village, after killing the leader of the Indians of Quarequa and six hundred of his warriors, Balboa fed to his dogs forty more Indians accused of sodomitical practices."[9] Goldberg discusses Peter Martyr's version of the story, in which the "preposterous" behavior of the indigenous people—cross-dressing and presumably same-sex relations—"infuse[s] Balboa's acts with moral purpose. It's as if he's righting a wrong."[10] Martyr claims that the slaughter was done at the instigation of other Indians who were disgusted by the behavior of their leaders. "After the forty sodomites are fed to the dogs, two kinds of Indians appear in the text, sodomitical ones and noble savages. As the latter lift their hands to heaven, it's as if they're proto-Christians, at the very least testifying to the universality of the Judeo-Christian condemnation of 'unnatural' sexuality."[11] T-Theology, which condemns same-sex behavior as unnatural, teaches Balboa how to justify his acts of brutality as, in a sense, acts of Christian love. That is the theology that Althaus-Reid stands against.

9. Goldberg, "Sodomy in the New World: Anthropologies Old and New," in Warner, ed., *Fear of a Queer Planet*, 3–18, here, 3–4.

10. Ibid., 5.

11. Ibid., 6.

T-Theology also functions by way of resemblance and sameness or, in its own terms, analogy. It looks for repetition, and it already knows what is there to be found. When it reads the Bible, it imagines that scripts and models for sexual and religious existence are there to be discovered. But such "resemblance hermeneutics" (hermeneutics refers to the interpretation of texts) requires participation in a process of abstraction that moves away from real, suffering bodies, which are particular and concrete.[12] Queer theology's departure from resemblance is also a departure from a God who is always more of the same, known in advance. Theology needs to be indecented, which means "doing a materialist, concrete theology which has departed from idealist grounds of understanding in a scandalous way."[13] Theology's false abstractions need to be acknowledged as abstractions. Instead of defending the abstraction of right sexed and gendered behavior by killing or punishing those who depart from such behavior, one must learn to recognize that God is in and with unruly bodies. Instead of defending the sacrality of property rights, one must learn that the kingdom of God is not about reward for hard work but about giving the same pay to those who worked a whole day and those who worked less than an hour (Matt 20:1–16). There is "no possible reflection on the alternative project of the Kingdom of God, unless the capitalist dictum 'there is no alternative' is also overthrown."[14] Queer hermeneutics, queer ways of interpreting and knowing, search for the alternatives that are already there and that need to be found. They search for the bodies in which God is to be found.

Of course, there's another sense in which T-Theology too is about bodies. Queer theology needs to tell the truth

12. Althaus-Reid, *Queer God*, 110.

13. Ibid., 35.

14. Ibid., 45.

about the strategies Christianity uses to deny its own investment in the production and regulation of divine sexuality and gender. Christian theology has often condemned any non-heterosexual-monogamous-lifelong-married sexuality; it also has a long history of speculating on what happened to Mary's hymen as she gave birth to Jesus (did it move aside to let him pass without rupturing?); and historical Christianity restricted the priesthood to men and valued the monastery over ordinary life. The indecent theologian thus doesn't project sexual images onto God. They are already there, put there by T-Theology. "Theology is a sexual subject; obsessively sexual in its interpretation of God's birth and parental relations; of men and women and their sexual ordering in society."[15] But, importantly, this doesn't mean that the "real" genders and sexualities of God, Christ, and other central Christian figures are lying around just waiting to be uncovered.

## REPRESENTATION, IDENTITY, AND THE REAL

Seeking to uncover the "real" is part of a search for identity, finality, and closure. An indecent or queer theology isn't only, or primarily, about representation as a way to find support for one's identity in God. This point is worth considering at some length. Althaus-Reid worries that God's identity is fixed rather than destabilized in such searches for identity, but searches for identity also presume the uncoverability—the abstracted or thingified character—of human gender and sexuality. In other words, the search for representation assumes that one knows what one is looking for and that what one looks for can be found. But if gender and sexuality are unstable practices, representation is not as simple as it seems. And if the sex-gender system as we know

15. Althaus-Reid, "¿Bién Sonados?," 56.

it is deeply distorted, representation may also participate in such distortion. As Halperin suggested toward the end of the previous chapter, that doesn't mean that the search for representation should not be undertaken at all. However, its good effects cannot be presumed, nor can representation alone be enough.

Thus, finding a lesbian God or a queer Jesus is all well and good as far as it goes, but the concrete effects of such images have to be explored, not assumed. Althaus-Reid notes that finding "the feminine side of God" repeats, rather than destabilizes, the core heterosexual masculinity that God is often given. "The metaphor of theology as the act of putting our hands under God's skirts belongs to another frame of thought" in which "putting our hands under God's skirts" is a way to "help us reflect on God in our lives beyond biological, parental metaphors or even dismantle—perhaps—the ghostly look of Sophia-Wisdom, and make of her an unreasonable, illogical God."[16] Looking for oneself and looking for equality in theology are not undertakings that bring us to a God who is a stranger, a God whose sexuality may be "closeted, that is, hidden and waiting."[17] Traditionally, Christian theologians have often emphasized that God is not continuous with our ordinary categories of knowing and valuing. God is *other*, and a God who is other may surprise us, rather than confirming what we already know to be the case. "Queer identity" too can be a search for finality. The objection here is not that people shouldn't understand themselves in terms of identity. Althaus-Reid certainly comes from a tradition of thinking about gender and sexuality that presumes their non-finality, non-fixity. That sort of position is not, however, about *denying* people their

16. Althaus-Reid, "Queer I Stand," in Althaus-Reid and Isherwood, eds., *Sexual Theologian*, 100.

17. Ibid., 104.

identities. Some people absolutely experience themselves as having fixed sexual and gender identities, and queer theology is not about knowing "better" about identity.

Queer theology seeks instead to avoid two particular types of dangers. One is the provision of sexual stories for others, the provision of what Mark Jordan has called sexual scripts that regulate how people tell stories about their lives.[18] The provision of such scripts can artificially restrict the way people interpret themselves and their behavior, but it also has the capacity to produce "good" and "bad" sexual subjects. This is most evident in terms of heteronormativity, but it can also take place in queer communities invested in "right" ways of being and behaving as a sexual subject. For example, in one context, the lesbian who occasionally sleeps with men might be considered a bad sexual subject because she isn't lesbian enough; in another context, the one considered a bad sexual subject might be the lesbian who refuses to sleep with men since she is too fixated on gender identity.

The second presumption rejected by queer theology is that of translatability or legibility. While sexuality and gender are intertwined in complex ways, one cannot necessarily be read off the other, nor can we assume that finding or inventing new sexual symbols in theology will free God. People's identities and sexual practices vary across their lives. Sometimes one finds oneself in situations, and relationships, one never imagined or expected: divorce, gender transition, new loves, non-sexual intimate relationships, sexual relationships without commitment or with different degrees of commitment, surprising attractions to people of unexpected genders or ages or experiences—all complicate expectations of stability and predictability in our sexed and gendered lives. Althaus-Reid holds that sexual stories

18. Jordan, *Recruiting Young Love.*

have to be tested for their effects on people's lives. Because human lives are always in movement and we never "have" ourselves in a full, complete sense, our sexual stories will reflect such movement in our lives. We are surprises to ourselves, and Althaus-Reid wants us to be open to such surprise. In T-Theology, she worries, too much is known in advance, and the same can be true of our sexual stories about ourselves and others. We "do not know what we shall be," either theologically or sexually, for "not all sex has a name or a date or place of discovery."[19] Althaus-Reid often expresses this unknowability by refusing the distinctions between what we sometimes think are separate domains. If representation, translation, and legibility were enough, Althaus-Reid jokes that she "would consider [herself] having fulfilled [her] duties as a believer and as a theologian by simply and only crossdressing Christ as the Virgin Mary" and by speculating about Jesus' relation to Peter. It's not that such representations of Christ aren't worth pursuing at all, but representationalism's assumptions around the stability, visibility, and legibility of sexuality are not flexible enough to leave room for a "strange God."[20]

Representation's reliance on symbols that can be read and transparently interpreted participates in a kind of symbolic determinism. The basic logic of symbolic determinism goes something like this: if we discover or construct the right kind of symbolism(s), right social order and right thinking will result. For instance, if we construe divinity as community rather than oneness, this will necessarily have socially salutary effects. Or, if we recognize that the body of Christ (the actually existing church) is made up of persons of all sexes, genders, and sexualities, then the body of

19. Althaus-Reid, *Queer God*, 59.

20. Althaus-Reid, "Queer I Stand," in Althaus-Reid and Isherwood, eds., *The Sexual Theologian*, 104–5.

Christ (symbolic and real) will no longer be masculine; it will be queer. Once we recognize that the body of Christ is queer, queers can then be included into the fluid and diverse body. The construction of such images to some extent assumes our capacity to know what effect our symbols will have, so that we can determine which symbols to invent or celebrate, in order to achieve the social outcomes we want. As we have seen, such knowledge depends on a vision of human beings as self-determining actors that is not in keeping with queer's (and theology's!) history of suspicion of the transparency of the self to the self. Because of her anthropology and her theory of the intertwining of religious symbols and economic practices, Althaus-Reid does not assume that either human beings *or* symbols work in the way symbolic determinism requires.

Thus, Althaus-Reid seeks movement and disruption.

> In a way, what we need is to recover the memory of the scandal in theology, and with a vengeance. This is the scandal of what T-Theology has carefully avoided: God amongst the Queer, and the Queer God present in Godself; God, as found in the complexity of the unruly sexualities and relationships of people; God, as present in the *via rupta* [the way of rupture] of previously unrecognised paths of praxis . . . The theological scandal is that bodies speak, and God speaks through them. . . . Queerness is something that belongs to God, and . . . people are divinely Queer by grace.[21]

Look at the sequence here, which is different than we might typically have expected. Queerness is *God's*; we become queer *by grace*. Bodies speak, and that speech is also God's. God is not a tidy God, categorizing God's people neatly and

21. Ibid., 33–34.

expecting them to stay within such categories, no matter which body parts that means cutting off (see Althaus-Reid's discussion of spiritual clitoridectomy).[22]

On a recent Sunday, the service at a progressive church I was visiting closed with an invocation that discussed how God is not only masculine but feminine too, nurturing, like a mother hen, like someone breastfeeding a child, and God does not have a penis. Indeed, God is not only masculine and feminine, but also a little bit trans, the minister said. Now, it was clear that the invocation came from a place of good intentions, but this way of finding identity in God is not that of queer theology. In the invocation, masculine and feminine are presupposed as settled categories. Femininity is equated with nurturing and the absence of a penis—which mistakenly confuses anatomy with gender and denies the complexity of femininity *and* masculinity, as well as the reality of those who understand themselves in nonbinary ways. In contrast, queer theology calls for "an omnisexual kenosis," which "is a melancholic art . . . [I]t represents a continuous attempt to understand sexual identities as a process consisting of the movement of emptiness not only of heterosexuality and heterosexual constructions, but of any other constructions of sexuality. For there are many longings of the heart amongst the nomadic people of God which go frustrated or even unacknowledged."[23]

Those of us who are invested in thinking differently about gender and sexuality can sometimes become concerned with finding the right story, the better story, the story that will allow each person in their own full sexual and gender identity to find themselves in the story. But no such story

22. Althaus-Reid, *Indecent Theology*, 49. For a view of the Virgin Mary that engages with Althaus-Reid's critique on this point, see Talder, "Our Lady of the Libido."

23. Althaus-Reid, *Queer God*, 57.

can be provided; we will never get identity "right." Again, Althaus-Reid is not denying the stories that people tell about themselves, but she does want to avoid locking down the types of stories available so that some find themselves unable to tell the truth about their "longings of the heart" because they don't fit into the narrative scripts at hand. The truth at stake here is not so much the truth of authenticity as the truth of complexity, of partiality, of existence without finality, transparency and self-possession.[24]

## BODIES AND ORGIES

Heterosexuality the identity and heterosexuality the socio-political system are both empty, but so is homosexuality the identity, or bisexuality the identity—but not bisexuality the *critical epistemological praxis*, bisexuality that reflects on its conditions of knowing. Bisexuality is "an epistemological identity" that doesn't assume "that bisexuality *per se* is a liberative force unless there is a critical reflection of its relation to other sexualities. . . . [I]ndependent of the sexual identity of the theologian as an individual, theology is the art of a critical bisexual action and reflection on God and humanity." Bisexuality is an epistemological position, which means that it's about a way of knowing, and a style of knowing, and a question of how to know. Bisexuality the *identity* may or may not be liberating: it all depends. Bisexuality, the theological-epistemological practice of thinking both-and and beyond the two, is a reflective praxis of liberation.

Queer theologians seeking theological justification for different sexual practices often reinterpret central Christian themes in terms of such sexual practices—for example, one might read the trinity as God the orgy. The three persons of

24. For a generative exploration of these issues through a trans* lens, see Mann, "'Queering' Spiritual Direction."

the trinity love each other with an everlasting, ecstatic, and absolutely joyous love. Althaus-Reid makes use of this image, but she doesn't just do with it what might be expected. One might expect her to challenge the restriction of love and sexual expression to just one other person, which she does, but that's not all.

"Let us reflect on orgies as hermeneutical reinventions," she suggests. At this point, she has reviewed the way sexual scenes in the Marquis de Sade's writings represent contractual agreements turned into sexual scripts in which different combinations are run through until their possibilities are exhausted. From such contractual agreements, or covenants, Althaus-Reid moves to "the covenants of colonial industrial landscapes," imagining the directions of export under colonialism. Yet resistance has never run according to straight lines on broad highways. Resistance requires different paths "cut out of the sides of mountains, or tracks cut through jungles, constructing new routes outside the logic of capital profit."[25] Althaus-Reid finds precursors to workers' unions in such forms of guerrilla communication. "We could call them perhaps, the orgies of the poor."[26] The orgies of the poor transmute into the Argentine Junta's restriction on illicit gatherings in the 1970s. Even Bible study groups could lead to arrest if more than a certain number of people were together in one place without permission. "From that perspective, their meetings had the quality of an orgy in the sense that an undesirable number of bodies were present in the same place under suspicion of producing unlawful exchanges."[27] The orgy becomes an imagistic way of tying sexual, religious, and economic practices together, reminding us of the many ways that bodies

25. Ibid., 31.
26. Ibid., 32.
27. Ibid.

resist narratives that depend on false abstraction from the messy complexities of our lives, and economic practices that deprive many of basic necessities while giving more to others than could ever be used in a finite human lifespan.

There is, we have seen, "no possible reflection on the alternative project of the Kingdom of God, unless the capitalist dictum 'there is no alternative' is also overthrown. That, however, would also require a process of disaffected investment in what we have grown to believe without questioning."[28] But let's leave Althaus-Reid's own language behind for a moment and tarry with the conditions under which such a statement might be true. It is here, I suspect, that some readers otherwise interested in queer theology might baulk. Capitalism can and should be made more just. But don't economists tell us that capitalism is the most efficient instrument of wealth-production, and therefore human welfare-enhancement, that the world has ever known? Doesn't connecting the reign of God to the end of capitalism reduce Christianity to no more than a sociopolitical program, better addressed by expanding voting rights than by rethinking God's relationships to bodies?

Yet Christianity is a story about God's incarnation, the making holy of the body, a story in which each person is the object of God's care, attention, and love. Christianity is a story of God's presence among the dissolute, and God's own dissolution (on the cross).[29] If Christianity, and more importantly, *Christians*, are serious about their claims, they—we—must be willing to reckon much more seriously than we typically do with their implications. The whole social order that separates people into the decent and indecent, that regulates accepted orders of bodily and economic exchange, is ruptured by a Christ who gave his life for all,

28. Ibid., 45.
29. Ibid., 29, 36.

but most particularly the despised, a Christ who died at the hands of a colonial empire. Althaus-Reid forces us to recognize that we're not dealing with a question of how to relate Christianity to politics and to the economy and to sexuality. Christianity is and has always been political, economic, and sexual. The question is this: what does an economy of infinite, inexhaustible love look like? Althaus-Reid seeks an economy of loving exchange, free gift-giving, and indiscriminate distribution, reflecting the economy of a God who distributes Godself among all people without reservation.

## QUEERING THE VIRGIN?

Having examined God the orgy, let's look at another example of what Althaus-Reid does theologically with the Virgin Mary. Althaus-Reid worries about the theological centrality of the Virgin Mary for women. Many theologians have argued that Mary is a promising symbol for women, because her virginity means she didn't belong to anyone but herself. Mary's presence at the heart of the gospel story means putting a woman, and pregnancy and birth-giving, at the center. Mary is a poor, humble woman, like the many poor and humble women of the world. But Mary is not really human anymore, Althaus-Reid says. She isn't a woman of flesh and blood upon whom one can pattern one's life: "No girl thinks, 'perhaps if I am humble enough God will have sex with me."[30] Yet Mary's femininity is relentlessly emphasized in theology: "the femininity of the Virgin Mary is consolidated every day by a theological citational process which gives human coherence to Mary, a humanoid symbol. In fact, Mariology creates a history of gender from an artifact: a supposed woman who does not have a recog-

30. Althaus-Reid, *Indecent Theology*, 55.

nisable sexual performance is made into a sexual code."[31] Mary's sexuality can't be imitated, since God-given, virgin pregnancies are impossible for anyone else. Thus the central theological symbol for women is inimitable, specifically in terms of sexuality and reproduction, two places where women often are harmed by gendered cultural codes.

In *Indecent Theology*, Althaus-Reid sees little potential for resistance in the symbol of the Virgin Mary. She simply submitted to God; she's the epitome of the decent woman. Marian apparitions legitimized the colonial conquest of the Americas and the military dictatorship in Chile.[32]

> Although Mary and Jesus' biographies are by historical standards very weird ones, Mary has more non-human characteristics than Jesus. For centuries, the Vatican has been building layer upon layer of what we could call proto-alien characteristics in Mary: first, the stone-walled hymen virgin conceiving by copulating with a kind of divine cloud and giving birth in some unimaginable way. Then, it was added to her biography that her mother was also odd in that same way, and Mary was also conceived from a cloud. . . . One can easily argue that the Virgin Mary is the strangest thing in Christianity and scarcely needs anybody to Queer her, but Queer is not oddity. Queer is precisely the opposite: it is the very essence of a denied reality . . . [W]e speak of 'Queering' . . . as a process of coming back to the authentic, everyday life experiences described as odd by the ideology—and mythology—makers alike. Indecenting brings back the sense of reality.[33]

31. Ibid., 53
32. Ibid., 58–59.
33. Ibid., 71.

Queering as a process helps us to come back to reality from the stories that theology tells us in order to make rather odd and inexplicable experiences seem like models for our shared social and sexual lives. But *Queer is not oddity*. Althaus-Reid here challenges some of the easy queerings of Christianity that insist that because Christianity talks about twists and turns and strange relationships between God and human beings, it is queer almost by definition.

In theology, Mary is reduced to her womb, but "the womb as a site for reproduction can be appropriated easily by the male."[34] In saying this, Althaus-Reid isn't returning to essentialized gender categories. Rather, she is concerned with (historically) male theologians' use of Mary's womb as an instrument for subjugating women. Male theologians offer Mary's womb as a pretend model for women, who should be humble and receptive, like Mary. And one ought not to assume that anyone who has a womb (symbolic or otherwise) is a woman. Althaus-Reid repeatedly points out that gender and (even symbolic) biology don't necessarily cohere. Instead, "indecent theologians may say 'God, the Faggot; God, the Drag Queen . . . God, the ambivalent, not easily classified sexuality.'"[35]

An undergraduate student, having read a little bit of Althaus-Reid's writing, once asked me, "If God has no gender, how can He be queer?" One might, of course, equally well ask, "If God has no gender, how can God be He?" But the parallel doesn't quite work, because for Althaus-Reid, God, like other fixed identities or categories in the theological imagination, needs to go through a process of queer-*ing*. God's queer "identity" isn't lying there waiting to be discovered, because the "queer" God might still be a "He," that is, an ideological support for heteronormativity,

34. Ibid., 55.
35. Ibid., 95.

patriarchy, and capitalism. A supposedly queer God might just reflect the concerns of some particular queer people, as when the "queer" argument is only about including people in vowed same-sex relationships into the church, or when it is reduced to a celebration of one's sexual practices, without any consideration of how those sexual practices are always part of wider sexual, economic, and racial systems.[36]

The abstract gender or symbolically sexual body parts of God, Christ, and Mary thus aren't Althaus-Reid's primary concern. Although Althaus-Reid does lift the skirts of God, it's not in hopes of uncovering a queer identity capable of supporting the queer identity of the believer. *Finding* sexual identity in God likely remains within existing categories of sexuality, which are not just categories of identity, but categories partly determined by their relation to heteronormativity, that is, heterosexuality as an ideological, social, and economic system of legitimation and recognition. (Again, remember that for Althaus-Reid, heterosexuality the *system* forces heterosexuals the *people* into denying the truth and complexity of their own lives as well.) What she is trying to uncover is the way theological gender and sexuality organize and value the lives of ordinary human beings, including their desire and their sexual relations. If we want to "indecent" Mary, that is, to find a Mary who would be for the poor, "her virginity is the first thing that must go because poor women are seldom virgins."[37] Mary's theological virginity isn't worth protecting if it comes at the expense of poor women, who are made theologically and socially indecent because they cannot be like the Virgin Mary. "The indecenting of the Virgin demands from us the integrity to stop the citational process about the liberative actions of the

36. Holland, *Erotic Life of Racism.*

37. Althaus-Reid, *Indecent Theology*, 75.

Virgin Mary and her standing for the oppressed,"[38] since her story is a foundation for, rather than a challenge to, theological, heterosexual, and economic codes of decency.

But can't the Virgin Mary be recuperated for women? "If Mary existed historically, then we can say with the Mothers of May Square that 'she was taken into that history alive and we want her back alive,'" says Althaus-Reid, adapting the cry of the Mothers of the Disappeared.[39] Theologians' insistence on recovering the Virgin Mary reflects not only her importance as Jesus' mother, but also the paucity of women's roles in Christian symbolism, period. There just aren't a lot of options: Mary, Mary Magdalene, Martha and Mary, Elizabeth, Junia, Phoebe, the Samaritan woman, the Syro-Phoenecian woman, the bleeding woman, the unnamed rich women of Luke 8, Sapphira, the Whore of Babylon—that covers much of the New Testament right there. The Hebrew Bible has more options, including Eve, Jeptha's daughter, Jezebel, the woman's voice in Song of Songs, the woman of Proverbs 30/lady Wisdom, the goddess Asherah, Rahab, Hosea's wife Gomer, Ruth, Tamar who slept with her father-in-law, David's daughter Tamar, Bathsheba, Jael, Delilah, Sarah, Hannah, Naomi, Lot's wife, Deborah—but even this very partial list gives one a sense of the *constrained roles* available for women in the Bible's symbolic world. The list above presents women as evil, whorish, or power-mad, women who want to get pregnant, mothers/good women, women who stand as memorials to the power of sin, women who are sacrificed for men, idol/goddesses, the good-hearted sex worker, and a few, a very few, exceptions to the usual roles: Jael, Deborah, Tamar's tricking Judah, maybe the woman's voice in Song of Songs. No wonder any woman's role, even one as ambivalent as

38. Ibid., 78.

39. Ibid., 100.

that of the Virgin Mary, becomes the subject of so many theological rescue operations.

We often distinguish between marked and unmarked identities, or the way that some social positions are taken as the default from which others are distinguished—think doctor vs. lady doctor in the past, or the way a character in a book is often taken to be white and male unless explicitly described otherwise. The actions of minoritized people are taken to represent broad cultural or ethnic tendencies, while the bad actions of white men are attributed individually: think of fundamentalist Islamic terrorism vs the right-wing loner like Timothy McVeigh. The Bible emerges in a vastly different cultural context, but it arguably shares this particular characteristic with ours: representationally, biblical men are varied, individual, and particular. Their narratives show complexity of character, motivation, and behavior. Like real people, they behave differently at different times and are made holy despite behaving badly. There is no story of a woman in the Bible nearly as complex as the stories of Abraham, Jacob, or David, or even as complex as the story of Absalom. Representationally, biblical women are mostly stereotypical, reduced to only one characteristic or desire, and quite often unambiguously evil and whorish, characteristics that are equated with each other. To the extent that we seek biblical models for understanding and patterning our own lives and behavior, and to the extent that gender is part of that search, the Bible doesn't offer many options for many sorts of women. Mary, who has a complex storyline of a sort, thus can hardly be evaded.

Mary, the theological simulacrum, the Virgin Mother, needs to be replaced with "Mary, *Queer* of Heaven and Mother of Faggots."[40] This Mary is a Mary of pleasure, "a woman who had 'seven times seven' clitoral sexual

40. Ibid., 63.

pleasure."[41] Recalling pleasure means linking love, lust, and justice together, as a basis for solidarity, empathy, and openness to reality. Humans are not fixed and static, and neither is God's storyline with human beings. At its heart, Althaus-Reid's theology is incarnational, about the presence of God in the body, the holiness of flesh. But Christianity, while always claiming incarnation as its central event, often seems reluctant to recognize the consequences of incarnation. As in the case of Mary, Althaus-Reid worries that the theological Christ has lost his humanity, his concreteness. Christ becomes "a God/man, a celibate batman, batteries included to supply his head with that halo of light which we frequently see in his paintings."[42] The central Christian claim concerns God's presence in Christ, God's presence in the body, yet the bodies about which theologians speak seldom seem to have much in common with the bodied lives of ordinary human beings (including those of the theologians themselves).

If, as I am suggesting, Althaus-Reid's thought should play a significant role in how we understand what queer theology can and should mean, we see that it should have the following characteristics (now again to schematize in a way Althaus-Reid herself seldom does): it needs to take the messy realities and complexities of people's lives seriously; it needs to stand against the distortive powers of capitalism and colonialism; it needs to express and honor human bodily being; it needs to get beyond the search for identity, fixity, and finality; and it needs to be about God's presence in, identification with, and love for the body, the way God calls us to bring love, lust, and justice together.

41. Ibid., 73.
42. Ibid., 114.

# 5

# QUEER THEOLOGIES TO COME

WHERE, THEN, DOES ALTHAUS-REID leave queer theology? The first thing to say: the question remains to be answered. Not many theologies have followed the paths she trod. The intersection between theology, sexuality, and economics has, in particular, seen less development than one would have hoped. Yet I remain hopeful about what can and may be done by queer theology. This concluding chapter considers several areas of interest relevant to queer theologies to come. The first section examines three promising avenues for queer theological reflection. The second reviews approaches to doctrines that engage queer theoretical resources in illuminating ways. The third considers queer theology's involvement with cultural and artistic forms. Finally, we consider whether, given the trajectory of this book's argument, the claim should be made that Christianity is queer.

## QUEER THEOLOGIES TO COME

The title of this section is misleading, in that the fact of discussing these theologies means that they already exist! I've nonetheless considered them here because they are either just beginning to develop, or because they suggest new or underexplored directions for queer theology. I outline, very briefly, a theology focused on relations with a planet at risk of destruction; a queer project founded on belief in Blackness as a possibility beyond resistance; and a queer theology that assumes the unconquerable, inescapable, division of self against self.

### Queer Ecotheology; or, the Divine Carnival

Many argue, with great plausibility, that there is no issue more pressing than that of ecology. How should human beings better relate to the world that surrounds them? Is there anything that can draw humans away from the trajectory they are on, which threatens to destroy or at least devastate the planet? And, if queerness involves thinking existence in the flesh, must not that flesh also be thought of as matter? Putting these questions together, we find something like a queer ecotheology, or a queer theology of matter. To take just one example, Jacob J. Erickson outlines, in several recent essays, what such a queer ecotheology might look like. In one, he begins (much like this book does) with Christian interest in the body in order to develop a "concept of 'theophanic materiality,' in which divine energy is entangled in the performance of indeterminate material agencies. That is to say [he helpfully explains!], I'm attempting to create a conceptual possibility for the queer intimacy of divinity and earth" in the context of the climate crisis.[1] A "theophany" is a technical term for a vision or revelation of God—one of the most familiar is the burning bush before which Moses was instructed to remove his shoes. So "theophanic materiality" understands materiality as a site for divine revelation, matter as that through and in which God can be seen.

Erickson discusses the work of an artist, Andy Goldsworthy, who creates art from the earth, rocks, cairns, and pebbles (we'll return to the significance of art for queer theology in a few pages). He also finds inspiration in historical Christian mediations on God's self-revelation in materiality, but worries that the historical tradition too often and too quickly returns to a division between an alive, all-determining Creator, and inert, determined matter. Such a division threatens to evacuate matter of any significance or meaning of its own. Instead, Erickson wants "a kind of queer intimacy" between divine power and matter's own energies: this means "to think of theophany as the transfiguring flow of divine energies in creation, reconfiguring the divine again" along with "the flow of earthy energies in the divine, refiguring the earth again."[2] Divinity and materiality are reciprocally entangled, touching. Seeing the flows of their powers in this way can help, Erickson hopes, to draw our capacities away from their colonization by capital's flows and toward action that will slow down or stop the planetary threat represented by climate change.

In a companion essay, Erickson develops these themes further in conversation with Martin Luther. Departing again from art (in this case a film by Isabella Rossellini),

1. Erickson, "Theophanic Materiality," in Keller and Rubinstein, eds., *Entangled Worlds*, 203–20, here, 204.

2. Ibid., 213.

he offers a "speculative possibility of flesh," a "flirtation" dependent on a "theological irreverence" that recognizes that it cannot revere, because "to revere . . . is to capture, to be able to identify the object of our reverence,"[3] and thus to be able to identify (and so to objectify, to categorize) all that goes into making our relation to the planet as well as our possible relations to a possible God.

This flirtation makes use of Martin Luther's vision of "creatures . . . [as] incarnational masks of the divine, divinity enfolded in the stuff of the earth." The creaturely is where God is revealed as hidden. This idea plays off Luther's insistence that God cannot be seen directly, at least not after the fall. Instead, "God envelops [Godself] in [God's] works in certain forms."[4] Because that is the only way God reveals Godself, Luther—in lines that I love—says that those who "said that God has eyes, with which [God] beholds the poor; that [God] has ears, with which [God] hears those who pray" are unjustly condemned. Those who approach God in this literal, material way are actually right because God says to us: "Look! Under this wrapper you will be sure to take hold of Me."[5] Lifting the skirts—the dressing-gown!—of God indeed! Erickson points out the "carnivalesque" character of Luther's writing, in which divinity, materiality, and humanity are wrapped together—as we take hold of God, who comes to us wrapped in a wrapper around which we wrap ourselves. That God comes so wrapped means too that we cannot be certain in advance (as Althaus-Reid always says) where we'll find God, or what God will look like when we do—or where God is to be found right now. "Creation," Erickson says, "is Divinity

3. Erickson, "Irreverent Theology: On the Queer Ecology of Creation," in Bauman, ed., *Meaningful Flesh*, 55–80.

4. Luther, *Lectures on Genesis*, 11.

5. Ibid., 15.

in drag,"[6] an image that can move beyond fixed visions of divine activity and created passivity. Rather than remaining tied to sexual-ecological stories in which the roles are already known and allocated, an irreverent, queer ecotheology calls us to move beyond the scripts we have.

## The Atheology of Blackpentecostal Breath

Ashon T. Crawley's *Blackpentecostal Breath* is intentionally atheological, for he seeks to avoid the enrapturement of categorical, or definitive, distinction that he reads as characteristic of theology and philosophy in modernity. Instead, Crawley looks for that which lives together in movement and breath, the "choreosonic." He defines Blackpentecostalism as "an intellectual practice grounded in the fact of the flesh, flesh unbounded and liberative, flesh as vibrational and always on the move. . . . The practices I analyze are a range of sensual, affective, material experiences: 'shouting' as dance; 'tarrying' as stilled intensity and waiting, as well as raucous praise noise; 'whooping' (ecstatic, eclipsed breath) during praying and preaching; as well as, finally, speaking in tongues."[7] To live Blackpentecostalism is to be "sent," set outside and "beside oneself in the service of the other" in "a critical sociality of intense feeling."[8] Crawley writes the flesh's movement, the sound of flesh, the feeling of flesh.

For Crawley, "otherwise possibilities" are always available, always present, alongside modernity's deformed regimes of racialization and violence. Otherwise possibilities are made available in and through sound, in

6. Erickson, "Irreverent Theology," in Bauman, *Meaningful Flesh*, emphasis removed.

7. Crawley, *Blackpentecostal Breath*, 4.

8. Ibid., 5.

particular the sound of the breath, hollering, and whooping of Blackpentecostalism.

> Otherwise, as word—otherwise possibilities, as phrase—announces the fact of infinite alternatives to what is. And what is is about being, about existence, about ontology. But if infinite alternatives exist, if otherwise possibility is a resource that is never exhausted, what is, what exists, is but one of many. Otherwise possibilities exist alongside that which we can detect with our finite sensual capacities. Or, otherwise possibilities exist and the register of imagination, the epistemology through which sensual detection occurs—that is, the way we think the world—has to be altered in order to get at what's there.[9]

An anecdote Crawley uses to show the already-thereness of alternatives illustrates one aspect of the promise of his project for queer theologies beyond apologetics. He expressed his frustration to a minister friend that people continued attending queerphobic churches when affirming alternatives are available. The friend answered that "the point of the work was . . . to let folks know that an alternative exists if they choose to join with it. And that idea has remained with me so many years later. Alternatives exist—already—against the normative modes under which we endure."[10] That already-thereness is central to Crawley's concept of the sound of Blackpentecostal resistance.

Crawley's point of departure is the precedence of Blackpentecostal modes of being—otherwise possibilities—in

9. Ibid., 2. Crawley recognizes that Blackpentecostalism is not "free of the problems of marginalizing," but he finds resources already within it that resist any such tendency (24).

10. Ibid., 31.

relation to the forces that then transmute the plentitude of otherwise possibility into resistance. That is, that which resists precedes and cannot be captured by that which generates resistance. Otherwise possibility is not reducible to resistance to stultifying normativities and fixed modes of being, but, in relation to stultifying normativities and fixed modes of being, otherwise possibility is also resistance. And for Crawley, attentiveness to otherwise possibility follows what he understands as "the affirmation of and belief in blackness," with belief being particularly important due to its religious valence in an era where the religious remains a figuration for what is suspect and non-integrable, particularly in its Muslim variant.[11] In contrast, the view of the world that whiteness has is "about the acceptance of violence and violation as a way of life, as quotidian, as axiomatic."[12]

A brief engagement like this cannot do justice to the vivacious capacities of Crawley's project. He traces a speculative connection between Blackpentecostal Shouting and Islamic practices of circumambulation.[13] The exhaustion that can be reached in the performance of the Ring Shout is a "choreosonics" that is about "being and sustaining undoneness."[14] In another chapter, he reads the biblical injunction to "make a joyful noise," as taken up in Blackpentecostalism, as "a critique of the given world, a political economy of austerity and exploitation. . . . That noise can be joyful is an important claim to make." Already in 1906, the police were called to investigate the noise the Azusa street revival was making, but "to rid the area of such noise would have rid the area of the flesh—black, white, indig-

11. Ibid., 25.
12. Ibid., 6.
13. Ibid., 96–101.
14. Ibid., 107.

enous, Mexican, Korean—that gathered together at 312 Azusa Street for their revival."[15] Dance, noise—these are the movements and sounds of flesh that has not yet been formed into the docile body required for capitalist performance and the ideals of heterosexuality the ideological system. Describing the choreosonic practices of antebellum slaves, Crawley writes:

> The vocable, the rhythm: both audible, both resonant, both vibratory, felt in the flesh, heard. The sound of the drum, the sound of the voice, the sound of the flesh when clapped, slapped, carries. But what is being carried . . . ? Is there a presence in the sound that bespeaks the condition of life, abundant life, that emerges within the crucible of enslavement, that is not created but rather rises to the occasion of brutal violence and violation? What is carried . . . is the sociality of otherwise form . . . grounded in the reality of its present moment, open to the possibility through the improvisatory use of imaginative faculty. And it was this imaginative faculty [that] was integral to the critique of the economic system of exploitation that needed their analog-organic flesh.

Crawley shows forth that which exceeds and escapes capitalism-racialization-heterosexuality the system's capacity to render identities into coherently regulated bodies. He writes life, writes breath. And in so doing, he opens otherwise possibilities for queer theology.

15. Ibid., 145.

## Queer Theology, Anthropology, and the Fiction of Invulnerability

As books and articles on queer theology proliferate, their methodological contours remain unclear. The mainstream of such work reflects the concern that many writers have to convince the unconvinced, or to reassure the convinced— hence the apologetic aspect of many queer theologies. Even theologies that go beyond apologetics often depend on assumptions regarding humankind and its possibilities that are not necessarily made explicit or defended. A fundamental issue remains to be clarified: what vision of humanity do queer theologians assume or want to promote? To illustrate the question, let's compare some telling anthropological statements.

> We humans are free only to be what we are: bearers of the divine image. Everything else is bondage, and it is this bondage from which incarnate Wisdom seeks to free us. . . . But of all the things that hold us in bondage, desire for our lover is the least likely to work us lasting harm. It is a form of love and as such is healing, lovely— a particularly potent sacrament of the eternal lovemaking between God and creation.[16]

> If we begin by valuing difference, fluidity, curvature; and questioning unity, rigidity, and uniformity, many of the doctrines of christendom become more open. . . . [B]ecoming divine cannot be a matter of being 'saved' from a wicked world or a sinful nature . . . [W]e might think instead of flourishing, becoming the best we can be. Flourishing, for a plant, can happen only when there is life and potential for growth from inside . . . Nor do most plants grow straight and rigid. Their beauty is in their curves, their

16. Farley, *Gathering Those Driven Away*, 3.

variety, the sheer abundance of difference. The divine is within and beyond us, enabling our flourishing.[17]

Those of us who already take up queer positions have some extra practice in the creativity and the cost of an aesthetics of the self. We are learning how to dig deep into our best possibilities.[18]

For gay men, men for whom desire for other men is something that is sacred, something which they resist any social pressure to condemn, something they can renounce only at the expense of personal integrity and, indeed, their very personhood, sexual desire cannot be but adventitious, something accidental, but rather is 'essential' to who and what we, as gay men, are.[19]

The first statement depends on a vision of a healthy sexuality, a sexuality that does not harm, or that at least does less harm than any other feature of human existence. The association between sexuality and health derives from what many of us would consider eugenicist associations between the health of the social body and the health of the individual body, which also carries with it the implication that healthy sexuality reflects virtuous personhood. Many would want to disavow that relationship, thanks to a recognition of the undesirable consequences of connecting the health of one's sexual practices to assessment of one's moral status as a person. Yet it is difficult to see how such consequences can be disavowed if and when the notion of healthy—i.e., not harmful—sexual practices exists in the first place. The presumption of their existence implies

17. Jantzen, "Contours of a Queer Theology," 278–80.

18. Ibid., 282.

19. Long, "Heavenly Sex," 36.

their choosability, their achievability. (Or, in the language of moral theologians: ought implies can.) The implication of responsibility for unhealthy sexual practices cannot but then ensue.

The second statement sees queerness as a practice of flourishing, "becoming the best we can be." (The author should not be held responsible for the echo of the old U.S. Army slogan, "Be all you can be.") Queerness is about beauty, variety, and creativity, about an intrinsic maximization of the self's possibilities.

The third statement invites a more direct contrast:

> The self which the sexual shatters provides the basis on which sexuality is associated with power . . . For it is perhaps primarily the degeneration of the sexual into a relationship that condemns sexuality to becoming a struggle for power. As soon as persons are posited, the war begins.[20]

> The self is a practical convenience; promoted to the status of an ethical ideal, it is a sanction for violence. If sexuality is socially dysfunctional in that it brings people together only to plunge them into a self-shattering and solipsistic jouissance that drives them apart, it could also be thought of as our primary hygienic practice of nonviolence.[21]

The above quotations come from Leo Bersani's famous and controversial essay, "Is the Rectum a Grave?," first published in 1987 at the height of the AIDS crisis, when the association between gay male sexuality and death was at its apex in the popular imagination. Bersani's argument in that essay, shortened and simplified, is this: sex, particularly in

20. Bersani, *Is the Rectum a Grave?*, 25.
21. Ibid., 30.

some of its forms, has the capacity to remind us both of our fundamental powerlessness, a powerlessness essential to bodily being, and of the value of such powerlessness. Sex overwhelms us; it removes, at least momentarily, our capacity to organize and control the impressions the world around makes on us. The experience of sex reminds us of our fundamental vulnerability, and by associating that vulnerability with pleasure, it can hinder or redirect the desires for mastery that are otherwise constitutive of subjectivity's being in the world.

Bersani's argument has been critiqued for its overreliance on particular experiences of sex (especially gay male bottoming) and the presumption that subjectivity must be constituted by a desire for mastery. Both those critiques are fair. But arguments like Bersani's are often countered by the claim that, while some human subjects may need to give up their investment in power (i.e., straight white men), others have power denied them, and need instead to gain a sense of wholeness rather than dispersal and fragmentation. I want to shift the focus of Bersani's argument slightly to suggest instead that what needs to be given up is the fantasy that someone else is a self or has a selfhood that is fully integrated, whole, and authentic, rather than dispersed, fragmented, or in movement.

In short, are queerness and sexuality about reckoning with the ambiguity of human experience and relationality and the inescapability of conflict and (a kind of) violence, even in the "best" situations and relationships? Or is queer sexuality about maximizing the good possibilities of human existence, possibilities that can be recognized, fostered, and developed? The juxtaposition of Bersani's claims with a quote that advances a direct relationship between personhood, integrity, and sexuality, vivifies the contrast here. For Bersani, the myth of inviolable personhood is destroyed by sexuality; for the author of the earlier quote, sexuality confirms and expresses personhood's integrity.

These differences are often evaded, but they should, instead, be discussed. Difference, as these quotations rather beautifully illustrate, is conflictual. Visions of fully integrated, nonconflictual and nonconflicted relationships among human beings are (at least short of the eschaton) simply false, I would suggest. Among contemporary queer theological projects, relatively few wrestle with, or stay with, the kind of anthropology implied in Bersani's essay. A project that does is found in the work of Kent Brintnall, which, like Crawley's, is in a close, indeed intimate relation with theology without necessarily limiting itself to or identifying with theology.

Brintnall worries about the social effect of visions of invulnerability or plenitudinous—that is, whole, integrated, non-ambivalent and non-lacking—subjectivity. Such visions harm, he thinks, all subjects, both those who conform relatively better and those who conform relatively less well to the (false) image of personhood presumed in these visions. Because such visions are particularly closely associated with cultural ideas of masculinity, Brintnall analyzes representations of suffering, broken male bodies in order to show how those representations can rob the viewer of what we might call delusions of grandeur: the illusion that one is not (really) oneself vulnerable to the limits of power, one's incapacity for reckoning with the inability of one's intentions to determine either one's action or its outcome, along with one's inability truly to identify one's intentions, or indeed to know oneself at all.[22] When the viewer encounters the male-body-in-pain—and the crucified Christ is a prime example of such an encounter—representations of the vulnerable, lacerated male body can, in a sense, generate

22. Brintnall, *Ecce Homo*.

or perform the necessary puncturing of one's desire to be an invulnerable subject (although that puncturing is never final; the encounter must happen over and over).

Meditations on the lacerated body of Christ may not have the desired effect, however, because the crucified Christ is, in traditional Christian imagery, resurrected. Instead of an encounter with a vulnerable, male human being who cries, "My God, my God, why have you forsaken me!," the resurrection turns the crucifixion into nothing more than another challenge for the triumphant, powerful male body to overcome, Brintnall worries. He makes this argument through a comparison of the resurrection with the cultural script found in action films, in which the beleaguered hero is beaten and very nearly defeated before rising, one last time, to conquer once and for all.[23] Brintnall therefore finds more satisfying visions of male vulnerability and brokenness in Robert Mapplethorpe's pictures, Francis Bacon's paintings, and Georges Bataille's writings.

Brintnall's critique of resurrection's dream of plenitude raises the question of whether and to what extent psychoanalysis—so extremely influential for queer theory—and Christian theology can be made compatible. Whatever hope of a different order the queer theorist or the queer theologian might allow for the future, there may be a difference between affirmation of finitude (as psychoanalysis sees itself doing) and recognition of the guilt of distorted finitude (as Christian sin-talk requires). For intrinsic to the very concept of sin is that things ought to be otherwise than they are, that the world ought to be or could have been or will be radically (in some sense) different from what it is.[24]

23. See Tonstad, *God and Difference*, 261–63, for a longer engagement with Brintnall's argument.

24. The two previous sentences first appeared, in different order, in Tonstad, "Perils and Promise," 53.

That's exactly the dream, the fantasy, that Brintnall asks us to reject.

These three directions for queer theology are far from the only possible ones, and it's not clear that their methodological presumptions are necessarily compatible with each other. I've tried to describe them in ways that indicate why such projects might be important to queer theologies to come, without papering over the differences. In the next section, we turn our attention to some examples of queer theological work that illuminate specific doctrines rather than possible methodologies for queer theology.

## QUEERING DOCTRINE: THREE CASE STUDIES

In this section, we consider three examples that use queer theory to illuminate or generate Christian doctrine.

### Case Study 1: Christology

In *Christ and Culture*, Graham Ward approaches Christ through mimesis (representation or imitation), touches, flows, and relations. Ward emphasizes that Christ can't be seen or accessed directly, in the way we might know some other things: he is resurrected and ascended, so our access to him takes place in other ways. Textual interpretation is a central way of approaching Christ. In reading the gospel of Mark, for instance, Ward points out that the story both represents Christ and seeks to elicit our discipleship, our own following of Christ.[25] The story represents Christ by telling his story, but it also represents us in its address to us as readers and potential disciples. In the story, we are caught up with and into a narrative structured by God's actions—yet God Godself is unrepresentable. Thus, the story

25. Ward, *Christ and Culture*, 34.

leads into a crisis of representation: the representation of that which cannot be represented. Learning how to interpret in this way, and being reformed by the story, are essential to the story.[26] Textual interpretation and the crisis of representation—the breaking of meaning as representation seeks what is more than representable, the way representation fails to capture aspects of desire and what it is to be human—are central to queer theory as well.

Rather than considering Jesus from the perspective of the union of his two "natures," divinity and humanity, Ward looks to the materiality of Christ's relations with others. He views Christ's body "as a mobile site for the production of desire and belief, love and hope."[27] Christ is not a story of the self-possessed ego; rather, Christ's story is one of relations, desires, and intensities, a story in which others participate and respond. Power flows out from his body and heals the woman who had spent twelve years bleeding. Ward's theology centers on desire, our desire for God and God's desire for us. In the encounter with the bleeding woman, Ward points to the decision and desire that bring the woman seeking healing into contact with Jesus. In touching Jesus, she initiates the flow of power out from his body. Their two bodies, always in movement through time (like all bodies), engage, know, and change each other through touch. In their encounter, they are transformed in an asymmetrical relation of exchange. Ward emphasizes the financial cost that her search for healing has imposed on the bleeding woman; through touch, she is freed of the endless bleeding that is emptying her of life and of money.

Bodies, as Ward emphasizes, are exposed, vulnerable, and mobile; they are sites of fantasy as much as intimacy, distance, and proximity. As bodies relate, they flow into and

26. Ibid., 51, 59.

27. Ibid., 61.

out of each other, they desire each other, and they come to know each other, without dissolving difference and distance into identity. The touch of flesh is also the transmission of faith and the creation of new possible selves.[28] It is as bodies and through bodies that we know ourselves, each other, and God. Most fundamentally, our bodies are drawn into the story of God's body, the crucified, resurrected, and ascended body of Christ. Knowing Christ means participating in his acts by "co-abiding" with him.[29] In co-abiding with each other, in Christ, Christians journey as "ensouled flesh."[30] The materiality that Ward describes is materiality in movement, materiality that carries different forms of meaning and significance even as those forms of significance are mediated by way of touch. It is what he calls, following Gilles Deleuze and Felix Guattari, a schizoid Christ "whose desire is liquid and viscous, passing through 'relationships of intensities' in a way that demands the surrender of the ego, of the subject-in-control."[31] When bodies touch each other, they constitute each other's embodiment: it seems "as if the body is brought into being by that touch.[32]"

## Case Study 2: Original Sin

In the chapter on apologetic strategies, we briefly examined the "gays aren't sinners" strategy. Because nonnormative forms of sexual and gender expression have typically been condemned on grounds of sinfulness, queer- and trans-affirming theologies often invert the argument to insist that queer, trans, and nonbinary people are not sinners. Eager

28. Ibid., 64–7, 70–74.
29. Ibid., 106.
30. Ibid., 103–7.
31. Ibid., 61.
32. Ibid., 71.

to welcome people who may have experienced exclusion and condemnation, sometimes even persecution, in religious communities, queer- and trans-affirming theologies have been reluctant to say much about sin. To the extent that they do say something about sin, it may be directed at non-affirming churches and theologies, or sin may be equated with the refusal to live one's authentic erotic and gender identities fully. Sin is alienating or even meaningless language to many; the language of ethics and justice is the more frequent vocabulary for judging action. Ethics appears to be about acting rightly rather than wrongly, while justice respects the claims of the other. Sin, on the other hand, is negative and stigmatizing. It appears to orient the vocabulary of judging action toward God rather than toward other human beings. Sin attaches to the individual and modifies their very being: a person who sins is a sinner. A sinner is a wrong-doer. The person who cares about ethics and justice is an ethical and just person, at least potentially. At a minimum, they are a person who desires just and ethical relations, even if they may occasionally fail at living up to those desires. The person who cares about sin is oriented toward stigmatizing others, or a person excessively devoted to examining their own conscience. They are turned inward, interested in blame. So, at least, the landscape of contemporary language and imagery suggests.

Might there nonetheless be something worthwhile in animating the language of sin for queer theological reflection? In *The Romance of Innocent Sexuality*, Geoffrey Rees goes beyond recovering the language of sin: he argues that original sin is a helpful way of thinking about human sexuality. Original sin, in Christian theology, is the term for the way human beings come into the world already shaped by sinfulness. Original sin is about a fundamentally distorted orientation that we as human beings have. We don't enter the world in an absolutely neutral way, entering into a free context where we may choose the good, or we may choose evil. Before we act, we are wrongly oriented, and the context in which we act is marked by the accumulation of sin—both the actual sins of ourselves and others, and the malformations theologians have taken to calling structural or social sins: heterosexism, economic injustice and exploitation, racism, militarism, and so on. Liberation theologians, who understand God's work in history as being on the side of the oppressed and exploited, for the purpose of bringing justice and liberation to the world, name such structural and social sins to help us understand that while we may not understand ourselves as sinners, we nonetheless live within, contribute to, and often benefit from structures that exploit others. But Rees makes use of a different, and much more controversial, paradigm than that of social or structural sin. Shockingly to most of my students in queer theology, he adapts the connection between original sin and sexuality for which Augustine receives so much blame in contemporary thinking.[33] Much like Brintnall, Rees worries about the effect of imagining sexuality as the site in which authentic personhood is realized.

As Rees argues, "The promise of intelligible self-hood is a necessary chimera in the formation of human community."[34] The social order necessarily generates such dreams of plenitudinous identity and transparent intelligibility. Refusal to admit the chimerical nature of that dream denies one's own implication in original sin, and it causes disengagement from the struggle to remain "aware . . . , as much as possible, of the continual shifting distribution of

33. For a development of the doctrine of original sin in relation to sodomy, see Tonstad, "Everything Queer, Nothing Radical?"

34. Rees, *Romance of Innocent Sexuality*, 216.

the burden of shame of unintelligibility."[35] That distribution is both enacted by the self and caused by changing historical dynamics, but it reflects sin either way. "Blaming others, by shaming them, is a means of disowning one's own responsibility for sin."[36] Rees's solution is to accept one's own sinfulness and responsibility for it, along with giving up any dream of an achieved intelligibility in a fallen world. Instead, one ought to seek "to redress the continually unfolding harms that ensue from the inexorable present reality of sin."[37] Such action is informed, from the perspective of faith, by the hope of the resurrection and the gift of an achieved relation to a God who alone can render identity stable and intelligible and community non-exclusionary.

Rees sees Christianity's emphasis on the resurrection, on hope for a different order, and the promise of identity in the life to come as resources that can spur free action. Giving up the dream of an identity fixed in and by sexuality permits "faithful responsiveness to God who creates."[38] The promise of resurrection and a transformation of the sinful self offers hope for temporal discontinuity, a difference between what is and what will be.

In one of the most suggestive but underdeveloped passages of the book, Rees describes the promise of "the fantasy of a communal existence where sex doesn't exist, where the fictional expression of the fallen self's dream of wholeness in a sex never arises, where the self projects no sex to image its completion, especially in another human being, instead finding that completion in God."[39] Heaven provides, Rees thinks, such a vision. Here, he departs from

35. Ibid., 215.
36. Ibid., 277.
37. Ibid., 284.
38. Ibid., 288.
39. Ibid., 198.

an exceedingly common claim in queer or gay-affirming theologies of sexuality, that sexuality's and gender's distortions will be corrected in the life to come as sex, sexuality, and gender are transformed into an even better version of what they now are in their fallen forms, that they will then realize their intrinsic *telos* (perhaps toward participation in a triune and relational God). Rees implies that sex and sexuality may not be perverted by the fall: they may be results of the fall. Now that's a queer idea![40]

## Case Study 3: Ecclesiology

In *God and Difference*, I develop what I call an "apocalyptic ecclesiology"—an understanding of the church that is not dependent on reproduction, faithfulness, or patriarchal inheritance, but instead derives a theology of the church from the consequences of the loss of Christ's ascended body. Churches that concern themselves with whether queers should be included often worry that including queer people is unfaithful to God. Such churches are concerned with faithful reproduction, which often takes two different forms: 1) faithfulness to established doctrine and 2) a concern for purity that expresses itself by determining who is allowed to approach the eucharistic table and how.[41] The bodily purity of those who approach the table rightly is connected to their right to distribute the body of Christ to others. In this model of the church, the task of the church is to remain the same, not to change—to reproduce itself by training its new authorized representatives (ministers or priests) to defend the purity of the faith and to practice such purity in their own lives.

40. The previous three paragraphs first appeared, in slightly different form, in Tonstad, "Perils and Promise," 50–52.

41. Tonstad, *God and Difference*, 258–59.

Such ecclesiological models have as a consequence, I argue, that Althaus-Reid's diagnosis of resurrection as a "repetition or vicious circle of sexual ideologies" is correct, as is Brintnall's worry that resurrection revives a vision of a triumphant human subject who can't be defeated.[42] Instead, a queer ecclesiological model should reject that kind of reproduction as well as attempts to keep itself safe from the judgment of God. Resurrection can, but need not, mean continuity in the way that worries Brintnall and Althaus-Reid, especially if the ascension is remembered. Ascension means that the body of Jesus is, in a sense, lost to the church—the church doesn't have it, so the church can't control who gets to be or who gets to eat Christ's body. Rather than identifying with an imaginary, undamaged subject (here my argument is influenced by Lee Edelman's *No Future: Queer Theory and the Death Drive*) that will be recognized by Christ because of one's faithfulness, Christians should distribute Christ's body freely for they do not know where Christ is (except that he is with those in prison and in need) nor does the church control the means of access to Christ.[43] Such an ecclesiology, which emphasizes that the church is the *target* of Christ's judgment, rather than the representative of his judgment, is a non-reproductive ecclesiology or an ecclesiology of abortion.

Other examples that could have been mentioned in this section include Amey Victoria Adkins's retrieval of the Virgin Mary's womb,[44] Elizabeth Stuart's essay, "Queering

---

42. Ibid., 260–64, quoting Althaus-Reid, *Indecent Theology*, 103.

43. Ibid., 268–75.

44. Adkins, "Virgin Territory."

Death,"[45] or Kent Brintnall's recent movement toward an apophatic queer and political theology.[46]

## THEOLOGIES BEYOND THEOLOGY

As we have seen repeatedly, queer theology is often done in and through engagement with artistic and cultural forms. From performance art to visions of the Virgin of Guadalupe to AIDS poetry to black queer science fiction to painting to photography, much of the most interesting work in queer theology takes shape in relation to resources irreducible to the usual theological texts and traditions. Gerard Loughlin's book *Alien Sex* brings together theology, queer theory, and cinema in exemplary fashion, while Althaus-Reid's writing constantly experiments with literary form, inspired by authors like Kathy Acker.

But theology, in a broader sense, is also done in and through a variety of cultural forms. As Brintnall suggests, "queer scripture" might mean "*The Well of Loneliness, Portrait of Dorian Grey, Rubyfruit Jungle, Giovanni's Room, Frisk, Stone Butch Blues, Angels in America*" just as well as the Bible.[47] Audre Lorde's poetry has inspired many a (theological or otherwise) meditation on desire. The London-based drag queen Virgin Xtravaganzah, whose videos can be found online, performs in character as the Virgin Mary, offering deeply theological performances that aren't reducible to "just" theology.

Or, in another example, take David Wojnarowicz's famous video, *A Fire in the Belly*, which presents a campy and dripping-with-symbolism critique of indifference

45. Elizabeth Stuart, "Queering Death," in Althaus-Reid and Isherwood, eds., *Sexual Theologian*, 58–70.

46. Brintnall, "Desire's Revelatory Conflagration."

47. Brintnall, "Review of Cheng," 309.

to the AIDS crisis, particularly on the part of the church. Using red thread to sew his own lips together, and to sew together a broken loaf of bread, interspersed with images of masturbation, the US-Mexican border, and a crucifix lying on the ground and crawling with ants, Wojnarowicz (like Andres Serrano's Piss Christ) presents a powerful rebuke to Christian discomfort with the truth of incarnation. In identifying bodies of persons with AIDS with the crucified body of Christ while indicting the church for its participation in the murder of persons with AIDS and its rejection of its own (returned) messiah who identifies with the least of these, Wojnarowicz's film riffs on high medieval-gothic representations of the suffering body of Christ, marked by wounds resembling those of the people for whom the representations were made (as in the Isenheim Altarpiece, where sick patients gazed on a crucified body marked like theirs). The church, Wojnarowicz's film suggests, denies, even murders, its own Christ when it seeks to sew together the broken body by excluding and condemning persons with AIDS.

The theological import of queer art is not always easy to grasp. Wojnarowicz's film has caused repeated controversy. As recently as November 2010, the Smithsonian removed selections from his film from an exhibition after William Donohue of the Catholic League complained that the ant-covered crucifix that appears in the video denigrates Christianity and intentionally offends Christians by placing the ants on a representation of Christ. (One has to wonder exactly what Donohue thinks happened to Christ's body while it was in the *garden tomb*.) The Christian supremacy Donohue's victory represents considers it degrading to Christianity to show a Christ identified with suffering, with the flesh (including sexual flesh). Queer art can challenge theologians to go deeper into the materiality of their claims, a materiality that, as Althaus-Reid points out, is often forgotten or rendered abstract rather than enfleshed.

Baby Suggs's invocation to love the flesh ("Here, in this place, we flesh; flesh that weeps, laughs, flesh that dances on bare feet in grace. Love it. Love it hard. Yonder they do not love your flesh. They despise it.")[48] in Toni Morrison's *Beloved* is often picked up by womanist and black feminist theologians, as is Shug's affirmation that "God loves all them feelings" in her relationship with Celie in Alice Walker's *The Color Purple*.[49] The fiction of Samuel Delany and Octavia Butler invites meditation on race, flesh, and sexuality, while Delany's memoir *Times Square Red, Times Square Blue* offers an elegy for public sex cultures that had the capacity to promote the "interclass contact"—important for democracy and social transformation, Delany says, and essential to resistance to capitalism—that is increasingly difficult to achieve in hypergentrified and hyperstratified social contexts.[50]

I'm tempted to say that this section is so short because there's so much to say and so much to recommend! I have students working on poetry, preaching, pornography—to name just a few—for queer theological purposes.

## CAN CHRISTIANITY BE QUEER?

The claim that Christianity is, in some sense, queer—or even inherently queer—is made with increasing frequency by scholars and church people who want to emphasize that there's no necessary hostility between Christianity and queering. Such claims are typically made along the several lines that we've encountered at various points in this

48. Morrison, *Beloved*, 103.
49. Walker, *The Color Purple*, 196.
50. Delany, *Times Square Red, Times Square Blue*, 121–28.

book: 1) Christianity is queer because it is about strange intimacies and transgressions of binaries; 2) Christianity is queer because it is about radical inclusion and love; 3) Christianity is queer because it is strange. But, as Althaus-Reid reminds us, "Queer is not oddity";[51] queer is a praxis, a project—not a state of affairs, nor a state of being or practical achievement.

Althaus-Reid's point leads us to ask a different question: is *anything* queer, in this sense? As at least one influential scholar in queer studies writes, "Queerness can never define an identity; it can only ever disturb one."[52] This is not, at least as far as I read it, exactly to negate the various ways in which people identify, and the utility of such identification, but rather to point out that identification is never complete, never unambiguous, never uncomplicated. Put differently, that with which I identify is never identical with myself, nor does it (because identification of this kind cannot be irreducibly individual) share the particularity that constitutes *me*, a particularity that itself is always in motion. If queer can only disturb an identity, rather than constitute one, then the fantasy of identification—the fantasy of some self, somewhere out there, who is invulnerable, fully recognized within the social order, not caught within the incompletions and disappointments that attend any human existence—is rightly named as a *fantasy*. As Brintnall writes, "The longing to name, to classify, to order; the longing to know, describe, understand; the longing to channel desire toward appropriate objects in a proper fashion; these ubiquitous human longings demand that we draw distinctions, adopt rules, impose prohibitions. . . . To be human is to participate in these practices."[53] Recognizing that there

51. Althaus-Reid, *Indecent Theology*, 71.

52. Edelman, *No Future*, 17.

53. Brintnall, "Desire's Revelatory Conflagration," 10.

is no invulnerable self out there, no self fully integrated within a social and symbolic order, frees one from the idea that reaching such a position is the goal of social action. But that recognition means giving up some cherished ideas of what it means to be human.

However, two significant issues remain, and they have to do with whether and when Christianity makes a difference. These issues, briefly encapsulated, are the questions of *sin* and *death*. For many, the sense that queerness is about disturbance, incompletion, and the non-transparency of self to self follows from beliefs about the nature of limitation in human existence, or the nature of what theologians talk about as *finitude*: having limits, having a beginning and an end, having limits to power and knowledge—limits that cannot be overcome. Queerness then *affirms finitude*: it recognizes the inescapable tragedy of human existence.[54] To live into queerness as disturbance requires, many think, that the most difficult aspects of human existence be affirmed, particularly the futility that attaches to the reality that nothing human lasts, for everything disintegrates in time and death. Christianity too affirms finitude as good, for God looks at God's creation and names it so. But Christianity makes two further claims.

One is that finitude is malformed at a deep level— malformed by sin. The tragedy of bodied existence is then not reducible to its futility. The tragedy is that within the complications of futility—within existence lived with death (and therefore the certainty of loss) as its horizon—there is still a kind of excess, or what theologian Kathryn Tanner calls a "surd"[55] (something that can't be integrated or explained): human sin. As a consequence, not everything

54. Ibid.

55. Tanner, "Human Freedom, Human Sin, and God the Creator," in Tracy, ed., *The God Who Acts*, 112.

that attends the limits of existence in the flesh can or should be affirmed, Christian theology says.

The second issue follows from the first. Christianity also declares that "the last enemy to be destroyed is death" (1. Cor. 15:26, NRSV). Theologians and believers disagree about how such a text is to be understood. Is what is promised here the end of death and the transformation of life? Does the promise mean that even that which ends is not ultimately subject to futility? Or is the issue more about a particular human relation to death, death is approached with fear, aversion, and denial?

Human relations to death are both utterly particular and deeply social. My relation to *my* death is of necessity utterly particular, yet any relation to the death of another is always inescapably social. Many who seek to affirm finitude believe that death too must be part of that affirmation: the attempt to escape, to deny death, is part of what leads to the intensity and ubiquity of violence in human life. But there is a significant strand in Christianity that, as we saw in the beginning, refuses to affirm death as such, and insists that there is something *wrong*, something that is not as it should be, in the subjection of human beings and all creation to futility.

Here, we run into an irresolvable dilemma, a question about how to understand the orientation of a life lived under the shadow of death. That question is the question of Christianity, and the question of queerness too.

# SUGGESTED FURTHER READING

## CHAPTER 1

For a brief overview of the history and development of queer theology, see Cheng, *Radical Love*, chapter 2. Cornwall's *Controversies in Queer Theology* is also a useful text for such purpose. Both contain very helpful bibliographies, far more extensive than the one in this book. Another significant overview of the field can also be found in Brintnall's review of both books for *Theology & Sexuality*. Schippert's "Too Much Trouble?" is also a good orientation to questions about the relationship between queer and normative ethical ideals.

Brown's *The Body and Society* remains a classic in its treatment of the complicated sexualities found in early Christianity. Early Christian attitudes to death are illuminated in Rebillard, *Care of the Dead*.

## CHAPTER 2

The bibliographies in *Radical Love* and *Controversies in Queer Theology* contain many of the apologetic arguments discussed here.

## CHAPTER 3

Warner's *Trouble with Normal* remains one of the best introductions to queer theory's worries about normalcy and normativity. Jakobsen's "Queer Is, Queer Does," which I discuss in Tonstad, "Ambivalent Loves," traces complexities of norms and normativity that queer theology needs to continue reckoning with. Halperin's "Normalization of Queer Theory" was an early challenge to queer theory's investment in its own radicality. Spade's *Normal Life*, on the trouble with rights, engages concrete legal frameworks.

Cornelia Fine's *Delusions of Gender* and *Testosterone Rex* offer accessible challenges to many supposedly science-based assumptions around evolution and gender difference that queer theorists also typically reject.

A different history of queer theory than that of many standard introductions to the field can be found in Hames-García's "Queer Theory Revisited" in Hames-García and Martínez, eds., *Gay Latino Studies*, 19–45.

## CHAPTER 4

For more on Marx, especially commodity fetishism—arguably the foundation of Althaus-Reid's understanding of capitalist ideology—see I. I. Rubin, *Essays on Marx's Theory of Value*. Guy Hocquenghem was an early precursor of queer theory and also an important theorist of the relation between capitalism and sexuality. See "Toward an

Irrecuperable Pederasty," in Goldberg, ed., *Reclaiming Sodom*, 233–46, as well as *Homosexual Desire*.

Althaus-Reid has many agenda-setting essays well worth perusing. The opening vignette of *Indecent Theology* is critiqued by Emilie M. Townes in "Marcella Althaus-Reid's *Indecent Theology*: A Response," in Isherwood and Jordan, *Dancing Theology*, 61–67. André Musskopf's essay in the same collection, "Cruising (with) Marcella," 228–39, is worth reading. Hannah Hofheinz's dissertation, "Implicate and Transgress," is a study of the writing of theology in Althaus-Reid. Hofheinz's essay "Voyeur Bodies, Liberating Identities," is a useful study of Althaus-Reid on looking; it also engages Townes's critique. Marcia McMahon, "Trans Liberating Feminist and Queer Theologies," in Beardsley and O'Brien, eds., *This Is My Body*, 59–68, builds on and critiques Althaus-Reid's theology from a trans* perspective.

## CHAPTER 5

A shorter version of Rees's argument about original sin can be found in Rees, "Is Sex Worth Dying For?"

Garrigan's "Queer Worship" is an excellent introduction to worship-related issues raised by queer theology.

The main suggested readings are mentioned in the chapter. Queer and Christianity can unite around one injunction, at least: "Take, read!"

For a controversial but very interesting overview of gay male cultural forms and their potential theoretical consequences, see Halperin, *How to Be Gay*. Rambuss's *Closet Devotions* reads poets, including John Donne and George Herbert, with queer issues in mind.

Brintnall's review of Andy Buechel's *That We Might Become God* raises some of the same questions about possible relationships between queerness and Christianity that this book does, from a different angle.

# BIBLIOGRAPHY

Adkins, Amey Victoria. "Virgin Territory: Theology, Purity, and the Rise of the Global Sex Trade." PhD diss., Duke University, 2016.

Althaus-Reid, Marcella. "¿Bién Sonados? The Future of Mystical Connections in Liberation Theology." *Political Theology* 3 (2000) 44–63.

———. *Indecent Theology: Theological Perversions in Sex, Gender and Politics.* New York: Routledge, 2000.

———. *The Queer God.* New York: Routledge, 2003.

Althaus-Reid, Marcella, and Lisa Isherwood, eds. *The Sexual Theologian: Essays on Sex, God, and Politics.* Queering Theology Series. London: T. & T. Clark, 2004.

———. "Thinking Theology and Queer Theory." *Feminist Theology* 15 (2007) 302–14.

Barth, Karl. *Church Dogmatics.* Vol. III/4, *The Doctrine of Creation.* Edited by G. W. Bromiley and T. F. Torrance. Translated by A. T. MacKay et al. Edinburgh: T. & T. Clark, 1961. Reprinted, 2004.

Bauman, Whitney A., ed. *Meaningful Flesh: Reflections on Religion and Nature for a Queer Planet.* Brooklyn: Punctum, 2018.

Beardsley, Christina, and Michelle O'Brien, eds. *This Is My Body: Hearing the Theology of Transgender Christians.* London: Darton, Longman and Todd, 2016.

Bersani, Leo. *Is the Rectum a Grave? And Other Essays.* Chicago: University of Chicago Press, 2010.

Brintnall, Kent. "Desire's Revelatory Conflagration." *Theology & Sexuality* 23 (2017) 48–66. doi: 10.1080/13558358.2017.1341206.

———. *Ecce Homo: The Male-Body-in-Pain as Redemptive Figure.* Chicago: University of Chicago Press, 2011.

———. Review of *That We Might Become God: The Queerness of Creedal Christianity*, by Andy Buechel. *Theology & Sexuality* 23 (2017) 182–86. doi: 10.1080/13558358.2017.1343566.

———. Review of *Radical Love: An Introduction to Queer Theology* by Patrick S. Cheng and *Controversies in Queer Theology* by Susannah Cornwall. *Theology & Sexuality* 16 (2010) 308–11.

Brown, Peter. *The Body and Society: Men, Women, and Sexual Renunciation in Early Christianity*. 1988. Reprinted, Columbia Classics in Religion. New York: Columbia University Press, 2008.

Butler, Judith. *Gender Trouble: Feminism and the Subversion of Identity*. New York: Routledge, 1999.

Cheng, Patrick S. *Radical Love: An Introduction to Queer Theology*. New York: Seabury, 2011.

Cohen, Cathy J. "Punks, Bulldaggers, and Welfare Queens: The Radical Potential of Queer Politics?" *GLQ* 3 (1997) 437–85.

Cornwall, Susannah, ed. *Intersex, Theology, and the Bible: Troubling Bodies in Church, Text, and Society*. New York: Palgrave Macmillan, 2015.

Crawley, Ashon T. *Blackpentecostal Breath: The Aesthetics of Possibility*. Commonalities. New York: Fordham University Press, 2016.

Delany, Samuel R. *Times Square Red, Times Square Blue*. New York: New York University Press, 1999.

Douglas, Mary. *Purity and Danger: An Analysis of Concepts of Pollution and Taboo*. 1966. Reprint, New York: Routledge, 1995.

Dye, Lee. "Why Women Love to Shop." ABC News, Dec. 9, 2009. http://abcnews.go.com/Technology/DyeHard/women-love-shop-men-don't-blame-evolution/story?id=9281875/.

Edelman, Lee. *No Future: Queer Theory and the Death Drive*. Durham, NC: Duke University Press, 2004.

Engels, Friedrich. *The Origin of the Family, Private Property and the State*. https://www.marxists.org/archive/marx/works/1884/origin-family.

Farley, Wendy. *Gathering Those Driven Away: A Theology of Incarnation*. Louisville: Westminster John Knox, 2011.

Fine, Cornelia. *Delusions of Gender: How Our Minds, Society, and Neurosexism Create Difference*. New York: Norton, 2011.

———. *Testosterone Rex: Myths of Sex, Science, and Society*. New York: Norton, 2017.

Garrigan, Siobhan. "Queer Worship." *Theology & Sexuality* 15 (2009) 211–30.

Goldberg, Jonathan, ed. *Reclaiming Sodom*. New York: Routledge, 1994.

# Bibliography

Halperin, David M. *How to Be Gay*. Cambridge: Harvard University Press, 2012.

———. "The Normalization of Queer Theory." *Journal of Homosexuality* 45 (2003) 339–43.

———. *One Hundred Years of Homosexuality and Other Essays on Greek Love*. New York: Routledge, 1990.

———. *Saint Foucault: Towards a Gay Hagiography*. New York: Oxford, 1995.

Hames-García, Michael, and Ernesto Javier Martínez, eds. *Gay Latino Studies: A Critical Reader*. Durham: Duke University Press, 2011.

Hocquenghem, Guy. *Homosexual Desire*. Translated by Daniella Dangoor. Series Q. Durham: Duke University Press, 1993.

Hofheinz, Hannah. "Implicate and Transgress: Marcella Althaus-Reid, Writing, and a Transformation of Theological Knowledge." PhD diss., Harvard University, 2015.

———. "Voyeur Bodies, Liberating Identities." *Union Seminary Quarterly Review* 64 (2013) 66–72.

Holland, Sharon Patricia. *The Erotic Life of Racism*. Durham: Duke University Press, 2012.

Isherwood, Lisa, and Mark D. Jordan, eds. *Dancing Theology in Fetish Boots: Essays in Honour of Marcella Althaus-Reid*. London: SCM, 2010.

Jakobsen, Janet. "Queer Is? Queer Does? Normativity and the Problem of Resistance." *GLQ* 4 (1998) 511–36.

Jantzen, Grace M. "Contours of a Queer Theology." *Literature & Theology* 15 (2001) 276–85.

Jordan, Mark D. *Recruiting Young Love: How Christians Talk about Homosexuality*. Chicago: University of Chicago Press, 2011.

Keller, Catherine, and Mary-Jane Rubinstein, eds. *Entangled Worlds: Religion, Science, and New Materialisms*. Transdisciplinary Theological Colloquia. New York: Fordham University Press, 2017.

Kerr, Fergus. *Twentieth-Century Catholic Theologians: From Neoscholasticism to Nuptial Mysticism*. Malden, MA: Blackwell 2006.

Laqueur, Thomas W. *Making Sex: Body and Gender from the Greeks to Freud*. Cambridge: Harvard University Press, 1992.

Long, Ronald E. "Heavenly Sex: The Moral Authority of an Impossible Dream." *Theology & Sexuality* 11 (2005) 31–46.

Loughlin, Gerard. *Alien Sex: Body and Desire in Cinema and Theology*. Challenges in Contemporary Theology. Oxford: Blackwell, 2004.

Luther, Martin. *Lectures on Genesis Chapters 1–5*. Luther's Works 1. Saint Louis: Concordia, 1958.

Martin, Dale B. *Sex and the Single Savior: Gender and Sexuality in Biblical Interpretation.* Louisville: Westminster John Knox, 2006.

Martyn, J. Louis. "Apocalyptic Antinomies." In *Theological Issues in the Letters of Paul*, 111–24. Edinburgh: T. & T. Clark, 1997.

Marx, Karl. *Capital: A Critique of Political Economy.* Vol. 1. Translated by Ben Fowkes. New York: Penguin, 1990.

———. *Early Political Writings.* Edited by Joseph O'Malley with Richard A. Davis. Cambridge: Cambridge University Press, 1994.

Mann, Rachel. "'Queering' Spiritual Direction: Towards a Trans*-Literary Praxis." *Theology & Sexuality* 20 (2014) 214–24.

Morrison, Toni. *Beloved.* New York: Vintage International, 2004.

*Obergefell v. Hodges*, 556 US 2015. https://www.supremecourt.gov/opinions/14pdf/14-556_3204.pdf.

Olyan, Saul M. "'And with a Male You Shall not Lie the Lying Down of a Woman': On the Meaning and Significance of Leviticus 18:22 and 20:13." *Journal of the History of Sexuality* 5 (1994) 179–206.

Partridge, Cameron. "Side Wound, Virgin Birth, Transfiguration." *Theology & Sexuality* 18 (2012) 127–32, doi: http://dx.doi.org/10.1179/1355835813Z.00000000010.

Rambuss, Richard. *Closet Devotions.* Durham, NC: Duke University Press, 1998.

Rebillard, Éric. *The Care of the Dead in Late Antiquity.* Translated by Elizabeth Trapnell Rawlings and Jeanine Routier-Pucci. Ithaca: Cornell University Press, 2009.

Rees, Geoffrey. "Is Sex Worth Dying For? Sentimental-Homicidal-Suicidal Violence in Theological Discourse of Sexuality." *Journal of Religious Ethics* 39 (2011) 261–85.

———. *The Romance of Innocent Sexuality.* Eugene, OR: Cascade Books, 2011.

Rogers, Eugene F., Jr. *Sexuality and the Christian Body: Their Way into the Triune God.* Challenges in Contemporary Theology. Oxford: Wiley-Blackwell, 1999.

Rubin, I. I. *Essays on Marx's Theory of Value.* Translated by Miloš Samardźija and Fredy Perlman. Delhi: Aakar, 2008.

Sanders, E. P. *Paul and Palestinian Judaism: A Comparison of Patterns of Religion.* Minneapolis: Fortress, 1977.

Schippert, Claudia. "Too Much Trouble? Negotiating Feminist and Queer Approaches in Religion." *Theology & Sexuality* 11 (1999) 44–63.

Sedgwick, Eve Kosofsky. "Paranoid Reading and Reparative Reading, or, You're So Paranoid, You Probably Think This Essay Is about

You." In *Touching Feeling: Affect, Pedagogy, Performativity*, 123–52. Durham: Duke University Press, 2003.

Serano, Julia. *Whipping Girl: A Transsexual Woman on Sexism and the Scapegoating of Femininity*. Emeryville, CA: Seal Press, 2007.

Spade, Dean. *Normal Life: Administrative Violence, Critical Trans Politics, and the Limits of Law*. Brooklyn: South End, 2011.

Spillers, Hortense J. "Mama's Baby, Papa's Maybe: An American Grammar Book." In *Black, White, and in Color: Essays on American Literature and Culture*, 203–29. Chicago: University of Chicago Press, 2003.

Stone, Ken. *Practicing Safer Texts: Food, Sex and Bible in Queer Perspective*. Queering Theology Series. London: T. & T. Clark, 2005.

Stowers, Stanley K. *A Rereading of Romans: Justice, Jews, and Gentiles*. New Haven: Yale University Press, 1994.

Talder, Sian. "Our Lady of the Libido: Towards a Marian Theology of Sexual Liberation?" *Feminist Theology* 12 (2004) 343–71.

Tanner, Kathryn. *The Politics of God: Christian Theologies and Social Justice*. Minneapolis: Fortress, 1992.

Tonstad, Linn Marie. "Ambivalent Loves: Christian Theologies, Queer Theologies." *Literature & Theology* 31 (2017) 472–89. doi: 10.1093/litthe/frw043.

———. "Everything Queer, Nothing Radical?" *Svensk Teologisk Kvartalsskrift* 92 (2016) 118–29.

———. *God and Difference: The Trinity, Sexuality, and the Transformation of Finitude*. Gender, Theology, and Spirituality 17. New York: Routledge, 2016.

———. "The Limits of Inclusion: Queer Theology and Its Others." *Theology & Sexuality* 21 (2015) 1–19.

———. "The Perils and Promise of Imagining Otherwise." *Syndicate* 1 (2014) 48–53.

Tracy, Thomas F. *The God Who Acts: Philosophical and Theological Explorations*. University Park: Pennsylvania State University Press, 1994.

Viveiros de Castro, Eduardo. *Cannibal Metaphysics: For a Post-Structural Anthropology*. Translated by Peter Skafish. Minneapolis: Univocal, 2014.

Vogt, Peter. "'Honor to the Side': The Adoration of the Side Wound of Jesus in Eighteenth Century Moravian Piety," *Journal of Moravian History* 7 (2009) 83–106.

Walker, Alice. *The Color Purple*. New York : Washington Square Press, 1982.

Ward, Graham. *Christ and Culture*. Malden, MA: Blackwell, 2005.

# Bibliography

Warner, Michael, ed. *Fear of a Queer Planet: Queer Politics and Social Theory*. Minneapolis: University of Minnesota Press, 1993.

———. *The Trouble with Normal: Sex, Politics, and the Ethics of Queer Life*. Cambridge: Harvard University Press, 2000.

Williams, Delores. *Sisters in the Wilderness: The Challenge of Womanist God-Talk*. Maryknoll, NY: Orbis, 1993.

Wilson, Nancy. *Our Tribe: Queer Folks, God, Jesus, and the Bible*. San Francisco: HarperSanFrancisco, 1995.

# INDEX

definition, 31–32

dissolution of, in the New Testament, 32, 41–42

heterosexuality/homosexuality, 93–94

inadequacy, instability of, 55–56, 59

nature/culture distinction, 51–54

and nonbinary identity, 2, 93

valuing one side over the other, 32

biological assumptions about gender and sexuality, 51–52, 99

bisexuality, as an epistemology, 94

black feminism, 128; *see also* Cohen, Cathy J.

black people, exclusion from the normative sex-gender system, 66–67. *See also* marginalized/minoritized populations

#BlackLivesMatter, 67

Blackpentecostalism, 108–10, 108n9

*Blackpentecostal Breath* (Crawley), 108

the body. *See also* desire; queer theologies; the resurrected body

Augustine's views on, 10

body-soul distinctions, 4–5, 119

changing views on, 8

and choreosonic experience, 108

denial of, and the fear of death, 9, 130–31

as fundamental to theology, 8, 75, 106–7, 120, 126–28

in heaven, transformation of, 40–41

Paul's views on, 8–9

physical vulnerability, Christ's mirroring of, 116–17

as separate from self/identity, 12

and sin, sinfulness, 130

as unruly, uncontrollable, 10–12

God speaking through, 92, and Ward's Christology, 118–20

bourgeois family. *See* nuclear family

breath, 108

Brintnall, Kent

apophatic theology, 126

on the human longing to classify, 129

on male invulnerability and plenitude, 116–17

on possibilities for "queer scripture," 126

and the resurrected Christ, 117, 125

Butler, Judith

gender as learned behavior, 58

*Gender Trouble*, 48–49

on the interdependence of binaries, 32

Butler, Octavia, 128

capitalism

opposition to kingdom of God, 96